Who Murdered Elvis? 5th Anniversary Edition

Copyright 2018 by Stephen B. Ubaney

All rights reserved. No part of this book may be used or reproduced by any means: graphic, electronic, or mechanical, including photocopying, recording, taping, or by any other information storage retrieval system without the expressed written consent and permission of the author and the publisher.

Be advised that the contents are also protected by the Writers Guild of America: registration 1942375. Writers Guild registration Inquiries may be made to.

Writers Guild of America, West Inc.
7000 West Third Street
Los Angeles, CA 90048-4329
Voice: (323) 782-4500
  Fax: (323) 782-4803

Additional copies may be ordered at:

www.whomurderedbooks.com
www.facebook.com/WhoMurderedElvis/

ISBN: 978-0-9882829-8-8 (Softcover)
ISBN: 978-0-9882829-7-1 (eBook)
ASIN: B07DCBNLDR (Audiobook)

Dedication

To the most wonderful parents anyone could ask for. You give so much and ask so little.

Author's note

My quest for the truth behind the death of Elvis Presley began in 2007. That was the year of the 30th anniversary of his death, and it capped the third decade of my total disbelief in the repeated and ever-changing story.

On this particular date I saw a startling set of televised interviews. The interviewer was questioning witnesses about the discovery of Elvis' body, but not one of them could agree on the simplest of details: the time of day, the position of the body, what color pajamas Elvis was wearing, or even where the body was found.

It is a little-known fact that Joe Esposito, when interviewed at Baptist Memorial Hospital on camera, admitted that he found Elvis dead in bed! How could this be? Why do none of these stories match, and why are they changing? When numerous inconsistencies in witness death scene statements on the simplest of details didn't align, I began to dig.

After years of researching, writing and editing, I published *Who Murdered Elvis?*. It was the summer of 2013 and I thought that my book would be the last word on the subject. I was wrong. In the five years after its publication more facts, witnesses, interviews, and incredible personal experiences followed.

Some of the events were so incredible that I couldn't help but update and rewrite the book, resulting in the new Fifth Anniversary Edition, that lies before you. With the release of this edition I now have over ten years of investigation into the death of Elvis Presley. It is my hope that you enjoy the book and appreciate the massive amount of work that it took to produce it.

Introduction

This book is presented solely for entertainment purposes. It is a creative nonfiction book that weaves a hypothesis based on years of researched facts.

Some of these facts have existed in other authors' works for decades and have been presented within this manuscript to assist the author, and reader, with the development of the storyline.

In order to get as close to the truth as humanly possible, the material selected for presentation dealt only in first hand experiences and were of the best 'source direct' content available.

While the best efforts have been used in preparing this book and the author has quoted several official and credible sources, the content is a narrative of those gathered facts. The author is not a professional law enforcement agent or criminal investigator.

This manuscript was written without ghost writers, malice or ulterior motives. The author's sole intention is to solve the long standing mystery surrounding Elvis Presley's death and not to discredit or defame any character in the manuscript's fact-based hypothesis.

The literary journalism within this manuscript has finally assembled a believable and final event out of the scrambled and conflicting reports repeatedly warped in the public consciousness for years.

Those who are thanked

Robert Nasca Esq

J. Richard Milazzo Esq

Gary White Esq

Those who are acknowledged

Suzanna Leigh

Jim Ostrowski, Esq

Debora Becerra, Esq

Mark Lane, Esq

Those who inspired

Gerard Crinnin, PhD

Mark Lane, Esq

Richard Hugo

Robert Nasca Esq

"Truth is like the sun. You can shut it out for a time, but it ain't goin' away."

- Elvis Presley

1
The Chronicle

"Now you listen to me; the only thing that's important is that that man is on stage tonight – nothing else matters – nothing!"

- Larry Geller, Elvis: The Last 24 Hours-

There have been thousands of books written about Elvis Presley. The majority of these books do little more than talk about his greatness and soft-pedal his tragic death. Although some are truly terrific works, most were intended to do nothing more than profit from the specter of the man and monetarily feast on his legacy. They ask no difficult questions and deliver no real worth.

This book, instead, was written with two purposes in mind – one, to dispel the myth and fantasy that surround this man's untimely death; and two, finally set the record straight. Elvis Presley was indeed murdered.

Since Presley's death millions of fans around the world have been expected to just accept what they were told about his untimely and very suspicious demise at face value. They were just supposed to repeat what they had been told and roll over on command. But after a time, even the most casual of observers would start asking questions. Questions that no one had answers to.

For me that day was August 16th 2007 – the 30th anniversary of Elvis Presley's death. On that date there were televised festivities from Graceland and another candlelight vigil as fans gathered at Graceland to honor their fallen idol. Tens of thousands of fans were gathered holding candles high into the night sky, filled with enthusiasm and sadness.

It was an amazing spectacle. People the world over, who didn't know each other, stood in quiet and respectful remembrance that was fit for a fallen head of state or a Pope. They knew then what we all know now; we lost Elvis far too early.

It was a wonderful tribute, with the exception of a startling set of interviews that soon followed. These interviews, broadcast to a worldwide audience, made little sense and left me with a brain cramp.

A reporter was interviewing the members of Presley's staff who were eye witnesses to the discovery of his body. One after another the television captured their short video clips, and none of their stories were the same.

In fact, the witnesses couldn't even agree on the simplest of details – what color pajamas Elvis wore, where the body was found or even what time of day it was. I watched these interviews in disbelief. How could these "witnesses" be telling different stories, and why hasn't anyone investigated these accounts?

That is where my journey began, a long journey, where I investigated what really happened and separated fact from fiction. This book, for the first time, connects the disparate snippets of information into a final, believable event. But before we investigate the answers we must ask the right questions. To begin with: Who was the real Elvis Presley?

The name itself evokes mental images of the glamor and excitement that embodies Americana. From curled lip to swiveled hip, no entertainer riveted his audience and changed the societal landscape like this one man.

Men wanted to be him, women wanted to bed him, and Hollywood lusted to invent anyone with such an intoxicating persona. Amazingly, Elvis Presley's lot in life didn't start out glamourous or with any variety of appeal.

The story of Elvis Presley began on a cold winter's morning. Vernon Presley nervously paced back and forth out front of his two room shack in East Tupelo Mississippi. It was shortly after 3am on Tuesday, January 8th 1935. The wind was biting at his face and hands and he was doing something that he rarely did - talk with his father.

Inside, five people stood around the bed of Vernon's wife, 22-year-old Gladys, as she began to struggle through a long and tortuous delivery. Her labor pains were incredible, and the 18-year-old Vernon was so nervous at the thought of raising a new baby he could barely stand still.

The little white hut, which had been built by his family, sat on a lot next door to his parents' house and had just been finished. Vernon, his brother Vester, and his father labored long hours through the Christmas season to finish the house for the arrival of the newborn. It was a raw but sturdy building without the luxuries of modern life. It was a basic structure to give shelter to basic people.

Without the conveniences of indoor plumbing or electricity the labor that Gladys was going through was taking place in the most primitive of settings. Her contractions came and went by the flicker of coal lanterns as the women went about their duties.

Jessie, Vernon's father, did the best he could to try and ease his son's fidgeting as they occupied their time in prayer. Occasionally the door would slowly open and the midwife, Edna Robinson, would ask the men to get additional supplies.

The chores of getting more water, additional coal for the stove or borrowing another lantern from the neighbors kept the men occupied as the doctor was called for.

At 3:15am Dr. William Hunt arrived, and he didn't have to wait long to begin his work. It appeared that the long and grueling night Gladys had spent was nearing its end. Time grew short and the men were called in from their prayers in the cold night air.

As Vernon and Jessie huddled around the stove and stood in wide wonder Gladys' pain, which seemed to be endless, gave way to the delivery of a baby boy. It was 3:55am and the gleeful young couple were new parents. The name had been selected long in advance: Jessie Garon Presley.

The joy in the room soon gave way to silence. The baby was motionless, and without sound. Soon the doctor had the unhappy task of informing everyone that the baby had no heartbeat. Jessie Garon was stillborn. Vernon collapsed in tears, but the roller-coaster that the young couple had gone through wasn't over. Moments later, and to everyone's amazement, the doctor announced that there was another baby on the way.

As the women scurried about their tasks Dr. Hunt spoke to the shaken Vernon. *"Son, you've got another chance here, and I've never heard of both babies bein' stillborn. You're a lucky man and you've got a long night ahead of you. Go collect yourself."*

Vernon turned to his father as they walked back outside. *"Twins?"* Vernon was dumbfounded. *"Nobody ever told us we were havin' twins. . . "* Jessie told his young son, *"It happens that way sometimes. You've been twice blessed son. Now all we can do is wait and pray."* The men returned to the frigid winter's night and Vernon returned to his pacing on the dirt sidewalk.

There wasn't room in the little house for everyone, and although the men understood why they needed to leave, they weren't very happy about it. Ten minutes later the men were called: *"The second baby is on its way!"*

After a few minutes of continued hell for Gladys, another baby boy was born. It was 4:35am. Screaming and twisting the baby made its way into the world, but still the room held their breath as they doctor examined him.

After a few moments he announced *"This little guy is fit as a fiddle. Congratulations, you two. What are you going to name this little fella?"* Gladys replied, *"Elvis." "Elvis"*, the doctor replied? *"Yes, Elvis, that's my middle name"*, answered Vernon, *"his name is Elvis Aron Presley."*

That's the story. That's how the most influential and famous man in music history came into this world; dirt poor, against all odds, and in a drafty little hut on the wrong side of town. There was possibly no one in the country less likely to be famous than a boy born in poverty, and from a tiny town that few people had ever heard of.

Exactly how he did it no one really knows, but I believe what helped him along the way was a combination of faith, skill and luck. Regardless of how it happened, it was, and it still is, the biggest "rags-to-riches" story in American history.

What the Presleys lacked in money they made up for in love, generosity and faith. The Presley family was very religious and regularly attended the First Assembly of God Pentecostal Church.

It was at these services, which were very musically-based at that time, where little Elvis grew up singing and twitching to the music. This is where Elvis Presley's met his one and only true love - gospel music.

They were a hardworking and friendly bunch and Tupelo was home to many of their relatives. Vernon was born in Tupelo in 1916 and was the son of a woodworker. When he wasn't helping his father at his craft he was a laborer and a farm hand. Try as he did, the limited opportunities in Tupelo during that time period didn't allow him or anyone else to gain much traction in life.

Like Vernon, Gladys was also born in Tupelo. In 1912 she was born to a cotton farmer and would frequently work for her father picking and taking on many odd jobs. In her teens she learned the talents of a seamstress and worked diligently to help support her large family.

By the age of 20 she was courting Vernon, a much younger man of 16, and wanted desperately to marry him. Unfortunately, that was impossible, as Vernon was still a minor. The couple eventually borrowed $3 from their friends, went to a neighboring town, lied about their ages, and eloped.

As a mother, Gladys was loving and over protective. She laid down the rules and was the disciplinarian if those rules were broken. Elvis' early years were rather turbulent due to the poverty and strife that he was reared in.

Although Elvis was the center of their lives, and they did the very best they could to provide for him, they barely got by. They often relied on help from neighbors and the assistance of government food. Just when the Presleys thought that life couldn't get any worse during the Great Depression – it did.

Desperate to make a buck, Vernon intended to sell a hog that he had raised for a tidy profit. He knew that Orville Bean, his landlord and farm employer, would buy a fatted hog for a good sum of money.

They agreed on a price of $14, and that was just fine by Vernon who needed every dime he could muster. When the hog was sold however, Vernon only received a check for $4. Vernon was furious! *"What is this nonsense?!"* Vernon pleaded with the man. *"This wasn't the price we agreed on, and I have a baby to feed."* Vernon's pleas were useless.

Vernon knew that he was being taken advantage of and decided to right the wrong. Talking the situation over with his brother-in-law, and a close friend, he decided to take matters into his own hands. Vernon placed blank check over the one that he was paid with.

He then traced Bean's signature, making the new check out for the correct amount of $14. Unfortunately for Vernon this $10 discrepancy carried with it a heavy price. On May 25th 1938 the three men were arrested for forgery and the court sentenced Vernon to the Mississippi State Penitentiary for a three year term, leaving his wife and baby without an income.

Within a matter of months, Gladys was evicted by Orville Bean, who, ironically, was the same man that pressed the charges on her husband. Nevertheless, Gladys, with no means of support, and with baby in tow, was homeless.

Within a matter of months Bean had come to realize the hardship that he had created on Gladys and little Elvis as he saw their suffering. He knew that it wasn't right for Vernon's wife and baby to suffer so badly so he started a petition for Vernon's release which was signed and enacted by Mississippi Governor Hugh White. On February 6th 1939, Vernon was released from Prison with a six month suspension of his sentence contingent upon his good behavior.

A short time later Vernon was granted a suspended sentence, but the damage had been done. He was an ex-convict with no job, no house, and no way to fend for himself or his family. While he was away another thing happened. Elvis had created such a bond with his mother that Vernon was treated almost like an outsider. It was this time together that forged Elvis' closeness with his mother, a closeness that would last the rest of his life.

Over the next several years the family moved from place to place, struggling to survive. As they bounced around Vernon ran a little moonshine and continued to take odd jobs to stay a step ahead of their creditors. He was a terrible breadwinner and was frequently away from home, casting the young Elvis in the odd role of "man of the house."

Many times during World War II Vernon was away from home working on one of President Roosevelt's federally funded WPA (Works Progress Administration) projects. The WPA was the largest and most ambitious New Deal program, employing millions of people to construct public buildings, roads and electrical grids that many people felt were necessary for America's future.

FDR enacted these programs to help solve America's struggling economic crisis as a large portion of the population was either out of work entirely or hard hit by the economic downturn. During these years Elvis was the only person that Gladys could really count on, and so their closeness and odd dependency on each other grew.

When he wasn't working around the house, going to school, or helping his mother pick cotton or vegetables, he would sing songs with his grandfather when he visited. 'Grandpa Jessie' and Elvis would sing many of their favorite gospel songs that they had heard in church, and it was during this time that Elvis learned to pluck and strum an old acoustic guitar.

Jessie was a self-taught singer and guitar player who tried desperately to help Elvis overcome his musical shyness. Encouraged by his teachers who had heard him sing in church, the ten-year-old Elvis entered his first talent contest on October 3rd 1945.

The contest was held at the Mississippi-Alabama Fair and Dairy Show. When it came time for him to sing Elvis appeared onstage dressed as a cowboy. The crowd loved this cute, blonde haired little boy who was so small he had to stand on a chair to sing "Old Shep." Placing fifth in the show was no small feat for anyone, let alone a little boy who was terrified.

Vernon, who had recently returned home from a solid week of work, wanted to buy Elvis a nice gift for his eleventh birthday. The economy had been steadily improving after FDR's death and finally there was a little extra money to play with after their bills had been paid. Gladys and Elvis' grandparents also pooled their money and added it to Vernon's savings.

Elvis liked the idea of a bicycle because he could ride it to school, escaping the long-standing embarrassment of having his mother walk him there every morning. Everyone thought it was a nice gift for a little boy, so on the January 8th 1946, Elvis Presley's eleventh birthday, he and his mother entered a local store named Tupelo Hardware to buy a bicycle. Once inside, the wide-eyed little boy beamed lustfully at everything his mother's $10 could buy him.

As Elvis looked behind the counter he saw a rifle. It was love at first sight. From that moment on there wasn't anything else he wanted in the whole store. His mother nearly fainted.

There was no way in hell the overprotective Gladys was going to let her little boy have his own rifle! Gladys refused, and the two began to argue. Elvis began to plead his case as the store clerk, a man named Forrest Bobo, immediately began searching for something to calm the little boy down.

Reaching in the back of the glass case that Elvis and his mother were standing in front of, he presented Elvis with a shiny new guitar. The guitar did the trick. Elvis quickly started to strum, and after a few minutes the clerk asked, "Wouldn't you rather have the guitar?"

Gladys, who was grateful for any distraction away from the rifle, immediately told Elvis, "I'll buy you the guitar if you want it, but I am not buying you the rifle." After a few more minutes, Elvis agreed. Amazingly, that $6.95 purchase would put him on the path of a career where he would generate billions of dollars.

Later that year, Elvis and his guitar would become inseparable as he took every lesson he could from anyone who was willing to give it. His uncles both played a little guitar and donated some time to his newfound interest, along with the new pastor at his church, and of course there was always "Grandpa Jessie."

Soon Elvis took the guitar to school with him on a daily basis, playing and singing through his lunchtime. His guitar literally became his best friend. By November 1948 the time had come for the family to say goodbye to Tupelo. Jobs were becoming harder and harder to find.

Vernon was tired of his endless cycle of unemployment and poverty, and he knew that he needed bigger and better opportunities. The threesome packed all of their meager belongings into a bulging old pickup truck and set out on the road.

Their destination was the closest major city they could find. That city was Memphis, Tennessee, and in a short hour and a half drive they arrived at their new home town. In Memphis the Presleys lived in rat trap boarding houses where they shared a bathroom with eight other people until the situation became so unbearable that Gladys begged Vernon to apply for public assistance.

Finally, public assistance was approved for the Presley family, and they managed to find suitable accommodations in a public housing complex named Lauderdale Courts. It wasn't a fancy place to live, but it did have two bedrooms and a bathroom that was all their own. It was rundown and had broken furnishings but with a tremendous amount of elbow grease Gladys made it a clean and livable place.

While his parents were adjusting to their new housing situation the 14-year-old Elvis was enrolled in a new school, Humes High School. The horribly shy teen was terrified at the size of his new school and the overall size of his classes.

He spent the first two years moping through the halls and praying that he wouldn't have to talk to anyone. He did this remarkably well. Years later, when he enjoyed tremendous fame, even his teachers claimed that they never saw him before.

During these years his main escape from reality were his comic books, his music, and his affection for movies. When he read comic books he imagined himself as the hero, when he went to the movies he dreamt that he was James Dean, and when he played guitar he pretended that he was any one of his favorites, from B.B King to Arthur Crudup. All of these people helped mold the young man into his future self.

By 1950, Elvis began taking his guitar lessons very seriously. He hit it off very well with a guy in his neighborhood named Jesse Lee Denson. Jesse was a good guitar player, and Elvis was eager to absorb every scrap of knowledge that he had. It wasn't long before the two had formed a band with a few other guys who lived in and around Lauderdale Courts.

The band wasn't much. It was just a few young guys with a good beat playing for whoever would stop and listen, but Elvis didn't care. He was honing his skills and learning to overcome his incredible shyness.

Finally, during his junior year, Elvis began to mature. He grew into a young man and began to lose his awkward shyness. For the first time he began to focus on his appearance. Although still lacking in assertiveness and self-confidence, his hair, his sideburns and his flashy clothes became the new focus of his life.

While everyone else was wearing jeans, mini-skirts, and sporting crewcuts, Elvis was walking around with a thick mop of slicked back hair. He wore fancy shoes, dress pants, jackets with loud colors, shirts with flipped up collars and scarves that he twisted into a makeshift ascot tie.

This was not at all the norm in the conservative south and his classmates hurled insults, apples, eggs and even rocks at the kid who dressed like a freak and played what they considered to be "raunchy hillbilly music." To say that Elvis was unpopular with his classmates would be a tremendous understatement.

Red West, who would go on to become a member of Presley's 'Memphis Mafia', recalled that he met Elvis in the men's bathroom at Humes High School. Red walked in to see three guys with scissors trying to hold Elvis down and forcibly cut his hair. With a few right crosses Red rescued Elvis, and his precious hair, and that started their long-lasting friendship.

It wasn't long before he approached his father, informing him that he wanted to be an entertainer. Vernon was less than impressed. He told Elvis in point blank terms: *"Son, I never met a guitar player in my life that was ever worth a shit, so you better start looking for a job."* Elvis did as he was told, but he never gave up on his guitar lessons. The job he took was the obvious choice for a boy steeped in dreamworld: An usher at a local movie theater. There he could not only earn some money and get his father off his back, but he could watch all his favorite movies free-of-charge.

While he was working at the theater, he became more star struck than he had ever been and became obsessed with watching the bands down on Beale Street. Beale Street is a street in Downtown Memphis which is about 2 miles long and in the 1950's it was paradise for Presley.

Not only was it within walking distance from where he lived, but the street was the crux of all the music clubs in town. There the wide-eyed Elvis began to soak up everything he heard and he loved every minute of it.

Too young to enter the clubs, he would be up all night watching his favorite musicians through windows, standing in doorways and desperately trying to sneak past bouncers. Every now and then he would find a sympathetic club owner who would let him in, but it was a rarity.

It was there, in the bowels of Beale Street, where Elvis discovered his new sound, eventually merging it with his childhood passion for country and gospel. He became so obsessed with what he saw in the clubs that he was often late for school the next morning, which certainly didn't impress his parents.

When Elvis graduated from High School in June of 1953, it was a sigh of relief. Elvis hated school and the cruel people in it. He even failed music. The only class he ever failed and it was his passion. That's how unpopular Elvis was at Humes High School. For Elvis graduation wasn't a "rite of passage" - it was an escape.

His parents saw it a differently. They were thrilled. He was the first Presley to achieve that level of education, as his father was forced to drop out of school in the 8th grade help to support the family. After graduation he took a few manual labor jobs that bored him.

He worked himself to tears on assembly lines, in machine shops, even going back to work at the movie theater for a short time, but nothing suited him. His father encouraged him to learn a trade to separate himself from being a laborer so Elvis got a job with the Crown Electric Company.

There he made deliveries, drove truck, and was in line to be an apprentice electrician when the universe had other ideas. One of his friends lent Elvis $4 so he could hear himself on record.

It took him several weeks to build up his courage but he finally took what he learned from Beale Street and Tupelo and walked into Sun Records. Sun was a local recording studio within walking distance of his house and the owner, Sam Phillips, was always on the lookout for new musical trends.

This was the moment that Elvis had been grooming himself for since he was five years old. Now he would finally be on record. After a few clumsy minutes he recorded "My Happiness" and "That's When Your Heartaches Begin." Both songs were favorites of his mother. Phillips was impressed with Elvis but wasn't convinced that he was the sound that he was looking for.

That day Elvis left with only the recording that he'd paid for and not much else, but what happened in the next few months changed the world. Regardless of what claims have been made over the years, the person who discovered the greatest natural talent in music history was Marion Keisker, Sam Phillips' secretary.

During that now famous recording session, she understood that Elvis had the perfect blend of styles to fit what Phillips was looking for. More than a year passed before Phillips finally gave in to Keisker's repeated attempts to put him on Presley's trail. Eventually he agreed to give Elvis some studio time with randomly selected band members

Phillips had Elvis sing a variety of old "staple" country songs that almost every artist at the time had done versions of, and the recordings were a disaster. The Elvis and band members had never met before and they were out of sync. Not only was that a problem but the sound was not at all what Phillips wanted.

Nearing midnight on the July 5th 1954, the disgusted band members were ready to quit for the night when Elvis grabbed his guitar and launched into his rendition of a song by one of his favorite blues musicians, Arthur Crudup.

The song, "That's All Right", was one of Presley's all-time favorites. As he sang, he began to twitch his legs, jump around, and gyrate the neck of his guitar as if he were possessed by a demon.

The band members chuckled at him acting like a fool and then they kicked in with their instruments. Within a few minutes the whole band was having fun and acting like a bunch of goofballs. They were a great bunch of guys who were just blowing off steam from the long and uneventful session that they were leaving.

Phillips was in the control room, and upon hearing this ruckus, poked his head out. *"What the hell is going on out here?"* No one had a good answer for him, as they were just goofing around. Elvis said *"We aint doin' nothin', just goofin' off."* Phillips said *"Well go back and start it from the beginning. I have to get this on tape. That's great!!"* By 4am the exhausted men had recorded exactly what Sam Phillips had been looking for.

Phillips and Presley were a great team. One had the voice, and the other had the creativity. Not only did Phillips have a local studio and many industry connections, but he took Elvis under his wing and taught him the production end of the music business, a talent that would benefit him greatly at RCA.

Phillips was also open-minded and wasn't afraid to tweak and fiddle with convention. In crafting his new musical style, which Elvis' voice was the center of, he strayed from the tradition of giving the vocals more volume, which was the industry norm of the day. Instead he pulled Elvis' vocals back, which blended him in with the other instruments and created an unusual echo on his voice. Sam called that echo effect "slapback."

He did this by using a tape delay and by running the tape through a second recorder head. The result was a new sound that no one, even RCA in later years, could copy. After two days of finalizing the production of "That's All Right", Phillips took his demo to popular Memphis DJ Dewey Phillips (of no relation).

Dewey agreed to play it on his WHBQ Red, Hot, and Blue show. Elvis was a nervous wreck and went to the movies to take his mind off the importance of his big debut. He was horrified of being laughed at and hid in the darkness. When the song hit the airwaves it was such a hit that listeners were calling into find out who the new singer was.

Bending to the increased demand of his listeners, Dewey played the record in a loop for the last two hours of his show because he grew tired of taking requests for it. With the switchboard lighting up the DJ called Sam. He wanted to interview Elvis on the air but no one could find him.

Finally his parents located him and jerked him out of the movie theater. Vernon grabbed him by the arm *"Boy, the whole town is looking for you. You'd better get yourself over to WHBQ in a hell of a hurry. That record is driving everyone crazy and they want to interview you on the air."*

Elvis ran to the radio station as fast as his legs could carry him. When the interview began the DJ asked him where he went to high school. When Elvis said Humes, jaws dropped all over town. Humes was a white high school, and everyone was positive that Elvis was black. At that moment people realized that the music scene in Memphis would never be the same. Musical segregation was ending.

The demand for Elvis' music was so great that in no time the group was back in the studio. After all, they needed a B-side if they were going to sell this record and Sam had the perfect song in mind. It was a bluegrass number called "Blue Moon of Kentucky." In three takes the song ready for production, and by the next week Elvis was being played on WHBQ again.

With local airtime becoming such a huge success Sam couldn't resist signing Elvis to a management contract, and by mid-1954 Elvis appeared on the *Louisiana Hayride. The Louisiana Hayride was* a radio show broadcast every Saturday on the AFN Pacific channel of the United Kingdom. His performance of "That's All Right" resulted in Presley being signed to a one-year contract for future appearances.

On March 3rd 1955 Elvis was on the *Louisiana Hayride* again, but this time he was on television. The show was carried by KSLA-TV, the CBS affiliate in Shreveport, and Presley's star was quickly beginning to rise. As a result of that show, Presley's act caught the attention of Tom Parker, a savvy music-industry veteran.

Parker had previously promoted Minnie Pearl, Hank Snow, Gene Austin, June Carter, Roy Acuff and even Eddy Arnold. He had many industry ties and had frequented Las Vegas with his performers when Sin City was a town of just 10,000 residents.

In 1945, Parker struck an exclusive managerial agreement with Eddy Arnold for a 25% cut of the profit, with Arnold paying the business expenses. This was a double-edged sword for Arnold. Parker was a good manager, but he wanted to control and dominate every facet of Arnold's life. Parker was also was selling merchandise that Arnold didn't get profits from and he was secretly managing other performers on his dime.

These side deals happened frequently with those in power at RCA, and although Arnold needed Parker's management skills, he knew that he was being exploited. While Parker transformed Arnold from a country bumpkin into a superstar with radio shows, movies, and appearances in Las Vegas, the two men eventually loathed each other, and their arrangement ended badly.

Parker saw Presley's mass appeal and knew that he had a cash cow on his hands, and the timing for a buyout offer couldn't have come at a better time for Sam Philips. Despite being very popular on the regional circuit, by mid-1955 both Sam and Sun Records were having financial problems and were in serious need of a cash injection. Elvis didn't want to leave Phillips, but at that time finances spoke louder than friendship. Parker offered Sam $35,000 to buy out Presley's contract and Sam certainly didn't refuse.

In the blink of an eye, in November of 1955, Elvis Presley and his contract were vended. Parker was pushy, brash and extraordinarily smooth. Elvis' mother distrusted him on sight and warned Elvis to stay away. A similar warning came from Eddy Arnold himself, but Elvis had stars in his eyes, and pockets that were both tattered and empty. Vernon didn't have stars in his eyes. For him they were dollar signs.

He wanted Elvis to escape the poverty that they were living in. They agreed that almost any deal that would launch his career and fill his wallet sounded good, and they persuaded Gladys to get on board with the idea.

Parker agreed to represent Elvis for 25% commission on all monies, and to charge Elvis for all business expenses. Parker also peddled Elvis buttons, posters and other souvenirs from his vendor's apron and would eventually conjure up huge side deals with RCA that Elvis would never profit from. Their agreement was a carbon copy of the agreement Parker had made with Eddy Arnold ten years prior.

Parker also performed a carbon copy when he started managing Elvis. He gave him the moniker of "The King of Rock-n-Roll" imitating what he had done when he managed Roy Acuff. In a similar con, he crowned Acuff "The King of Country Music" before the world and to the adulation of his adoring fans.

From the first minute of Parker's management over Presley, things would be different than they were under Sam Phillips. Parker never let Elvis do interviews and intentionally kept him away from TV talk shows which turned Elvis into an object of limitless hidden fantasy.

The control over interviews made Elvis more exotic, mysterious, and obscure. It also forced fans to pay a handsome sum to see him. By 1956 Elvis and Parker had signed a contract with the William Morris talent agency under the major recording label of RCA and the worlds of race, culture and music were about to change forever. It was not smooth sailing as Presley's bump-and-grind style outraged conservative America.

Later that year a Florida judge declared that Presley's music undermined the youth of America as his gyrations were viewed as "a self-gratifying striptease with clothes on". In many cases, he was seen as a savage, depraved, sexual pervert and Colonel Parker knew it would only be a matter of time before Elvis Presley's life would be threatened, and it was.

Amazingly, the same FBI that had carefully monitored Presley's every move to protect the general public against this "vulgar" new star had now been called upon to protect him from assassination. The bull's-eye on Elvis became larger every day as a portion of society rallied against this obscene and radical new music that had hijacked the innocence of the American youth.

Despite the attempts by judges, parents and the sensational tales planted by the FBI to vilify Elvis' character, it appeared that nothing could stop the rising star – a rise driven, in part, by Colonel Parker's behind-the-scenes manipulation.

Beyond the resistance of black disc jockeys who didn't want to play a record by a "white boy" because he'd been accused of "stealing" black rhythm-and-blues, and the full-scale rebuke of conservative adults who rejected the image of teenage rock-n-roll rebellion, more sinister factors were at work. Parker understood the sinister undertow of the music business and knew how to manipulate the players.

In the same way that fight promoters own the top contenders that other fighters must face to become a champion, the Mafia owned the entire entertainment industry and the price tag attached to any climb toward stardom.

In 1958, while under contract with Paramount Pictures for seven pictures, and in the midst of shooting his fourth feature film, King Creole, Elvis received a letter from the Memphis draft board, ordering him to report for service in the US Army.

Panic-stricken with fear that they'd be sued by the movie studio for breach of contract, Colonel Parker pulled every string possible to get the Army to grant Elvis a 60-day extension to complete the film.

A "favor" from the US Army was as impossible then as it is today, but Parker's contacts completed this seemingly impossible task a mere 16 days after the letter was opened.

Nowhere in the US government does business happen so swiftly without incredible pull, and Tom Parker had it. He asked precious favors from people in very high places, and those favors would have to be paid back at a time of their choosing.

Elvis, like the rest of the American public, was totally unaware that the CIA and FBI were deeply involved in various domestic programs that murdered or removed anyone whom they felt pushed the government or society along an ill-favored path.

With the Cold War just beginning, the CIA had launched many new projects to ward off the Red Scare of Communism in the United States. Programs such as Operation Chaos, The Merrimac and various other Resistance Programs were designed and used to infiltrate, disrupt and destroy dissident groups by any means necessary. Mark Zepezauer writes about such projects in his book *The CIA's Greatest Hits*: "...the CIA used its domestic organizations to spy on thousands of US citizens whose only crime was disagreeing with their government's policies."

These programs were not the work of conspiracy theorists, or the fantasies of those with overactive imaginations. They actually existed for a specific purpose (and I tremble to think of what might exist today). To those in power, it was cheap insurance to preserve the nation's agenda and keep everyone on the same page.

Even today the US government's population is viewed as "inventory". In fact, "inventory" is the exact word that the IRS (Internal Revenue System) uses to refer to the American people. In that sense we are nameless and faceless. We are merely masses of people to be organized and manipulated away from major uprisings that could alter and damage the nation.

While it was true that the government would have to break a few constitutional laws, target certain groups and even murder a few citizens, they viewed it as a small price to pay for delivering control to the general public and maintaining order. A perfect example was the murder of Malcom X by the FBI for his connection with the black militant group, the Black Panthers.

In the mid-1960's the US government was horrified at the power that Black Panthers had, and they viewed the murder of their recruitment mouthpiece, Malcom X, as a small price to pay to maintain order. In the government's eyes they were doing nothing more than "managing their inventory."

While Elvis Presley wasn't Stalin, Malcom X, or public enemy No. 1, he had managed to gyrate himself to the full attention of the FBI as his stage hysteria was deemed a danger. Parents and teachers were outraged and complained to the TV networks in droves. They wanted him off camera!

Churches were no salvation for Elvis either. Religious organizations across the nation assembled themselves to burn and break his records. They even boycotted the record stores that sold them.

The governmental powers had no choice but to act in a way that would ease the uproar to their inventory. The only logical thing for them to do was to find a way to get Elvis out of society, and drafting him in the Army was the answer. It was the path of least resistance for the bureau to manage their inventory.

Besides, back in 1958, sending someone to Germany to serve in the Army was the equivalent of sending them to another planet, which more than solved the FBI's issue with Presley. They saw him as a musical fad, and they thought he'd fizzle out, but there was another side to the story.

At that time in our nation's history, organized crime was as dominant behind the scenes in the entertainment industry as it was in the US government. The brains behind their outfit knew that sending Elvis a draft notice while he was under contract and in the midst of filming a movie would put him in an obvious breach of contract with Paramount Pictures. This was no accident, it was a trap.

They knew that this would pinch Tom Parker into a desperate move and he'd run to the mob and ask for powerful favors, which he did. The trap was set to perfection as this well-planned maneuver put Elvis, and more importantly, Tom Parker, in their debt.

For many reasons, drafting Elvis in the Army worked for both the mob and the government, and the two definitely weren't strangers. Drafting Elvis to soothe society's uproar worked so well that it was repeated years later. In 1964 Cassius Clay defeated "Sonny" Liston and won the Heavyweight Championship of the World.

Days later, Clay informed the press that he'd converted to the Nation of Islam and his new name was Muhammad Ali. The Nation of Islam, at that time, was well connected to the militant group the Black Panthers, who were creating a great deal of unrest for the FBI.

Who was Muhammad Ali's best friend at that time? Malcom X. Once it went public that Clay was now Muhammad Ali, he was immediately "reclassified" and drafted into the US Army to remove him from society. Clay was removed from society one way, and Malcom X was removed from society another way. In the same way that Tom Parker had honed his skills to perfection on Eddy Arnold, the FBI had honed their skills with the drafting of Elvis.

Being drafted into the Army was rough for Elvis, but it was nothing compared to what he was about to go through. What he valued more than his freedom or his music was his mother, and he was about to lose all three. The overprotective Gladys was having problems coping with her son's fame, his recent draft notice, and her marital problems. In order to calm her nerves she increased her alcohol intake.

She was also bending to Tom Parker's demands for her to take diet pills to help her shed unwanted pounds so she could appear in photos with Elvis. This was something that Parker had previously refused to allow because he thought that his fat mother would be bad for his image.

This tormented her liver into dysfunction and finally failure. While Elvis was stationed in Germany she collapsed during a heated argument with Vernon and was rushed to the hospital.

Elvis left Germany only to see his ailing mother die the next day from Cirrhosis. The official cause of her death was listed as a heart attack, but Elvis refused to entertain the mention of an autopsy.

Elvis was crushed, and collapsed several times before, during, and after the funeral, finally having to be sedated by a doctor. Parker had his hands full. Handling Elvis' business affairs and maintaining his country-boy image before a general public that once called him "a savage" was no easy task, but when he got wind that the heartbroken Elvis was courting a 14-year-old girl named Priscilla while he was stationed in Germany, and that she was the daughter of a career officer in the Air Force, he turned irate.

Parker knew a disaster when he saw one, and he knew that even the slightest hint of Elvis' pedophilia would end his career and the honest image that took so much effort to create. Parker reminded them that the same thing had happened years earlier to another Rock-n-Roll star, Jerry Lee Lewis, as the mention of him dating a teenager ruined him.

There was no guesswork surrounding the issue: Parker knew damage control was needed immediately to safeguard the star's reputation. To accomplish this lofty goal, Parker needed to control the release of information in the entertainment industry, which put him face-to-face, once again, with the only source that controlled it, the Mob.

Once again they had saved Elvis Presley, but debts were mounting. After his release from the Army, a brokenhearted Elvis returned to Graceland in a deep state of depression. Much to Elvis' misery, Vernon had already remarried a woman named Dee Stanley.

Dee and her three small sons: Billy, Ricky and David, would be moving into Graceland along with his high school friends Lamar Fike, Red West, Sonny West, his cousin Billy Smith. Joining Elvis at Graceland, for the first time were Elvis' Army buddies, Charlie Hodge, Joe Esposito, and Marty Lacker. The face of Graceland was indeed changing.

His new group of best friends and confidants later came to be known as the "Memphis Mafia" – a term coined by a photographer as they were seen driving up to Las Vegas hotels in suits, sunglasses and limousines.

Although the term was nothing more a funny tag that labeled Presley's loyal friends and employees, the real Mafia didn't like the term at all. Even the hint of Elvis' connection with the Mafia would start people digging for answers, and who knew what they'd find. Elvis and his family weren't thrilled with the moniker either. Back in those days there was real investigative journalism, and if they got wind of a story, they would spend weeks or even months digging into it.

Unlike today, where the news has largely become a society of canaries, repeating what they have been told to say by their political party or their corporate masters. Back then the journalism wasn't show business, it was serious business.

Back at Graceland, Elvis and his new band of brothers were settling in nicely. He had somewhat come to grips with the death of his mother and soon his cronies were lifting his spirits with practical jokes.

This 24-hour tomfoolery was despised by Parker, who distrusted these new friends and saw them as "hangers-on" who surrounded the star with unhealthy influences.

Eventually each was given a job necessary to the business, and the situation eased. Since the friends weren't on Parker's payroll and they helped with the function of the business, they were eventually accepted by Parker, but in his mind, they were always kept at arm's length. The exception was Joe Esposito.

By 1960, the time had come for Elvis to appear on television again, and Tom Parker received a call from those who held the organized crime strings in the entertainment industry. Their favorite son, Frank Sinatra, had teamed up with ABC and Timex for a four show special and the series was in trouble. Sinatra's first three shows had flopped and this, his fourth and final show, needed to be a hit.

The long-awaited return of Elvis Presley was a guaranteed ratings grab and Parker owed the mob a favor, so Elvis appeared for the first time in 3 years at a much reduced rate. The show was a great success, with 41.5% of the ratings, as everyone clamored for a look at *"the cleaned-up Elvis"* who was fresh out of the Army.

Elvis Presley and Frank Sinatra shared a checkered past. When Elvis first appeared on the music scene, Sinatra was less than kind to him in saying *"His kind of music is deplorable,"* and that it was *"A rancid-smelling aphrodisiac."*

The public was surprised to see the two of them together looking like old friends, but to anyone who knew what was really going on, it was no surprise at all. Elvis and Frank were both owned by the same people.

It was during this time that rumors began to circulate that Elvis was dating Nancy Sinatra, another clever ploy by Tom Parker. That way, even if news of Priscilla were leaked, it wouldn't have been believed.

The connection between Frank Sinatra, Tom Parker, Elvis Presley and Mafia crime bosses was very real and cannot be overemphasized. So real, in fact, that Sinatra's FBI file is a whopping 2,403 pages in length and the verbiage is peppered with associations to organized-crime figures.

For those of us who were born after 'The Good Old Days" and have no recollection of the way America really functioned, it could be easily said that a handful of men and their minions ran America from behind the scenes.

They could make or break movie stars and politicians at will. Once upon a time they could fix any sports event and were quite competent at running casinos and major industries.

These men were intelligent and powerful, and for the most part kept very silent. Frank Sinatra and Elvis Presley were the two biggest acts in American history, and they were huge cash cows.

There was simply no way their management would be allowed to stray, as they were nothing short of obedient servants to the powers that made and kept them.

Immediately after the *"Welcome Home"* television appearance with Frank Sinatra, Elvis was commanded to star in as many motion pictures as humanly possible to fulfill his "contract" and quickly sign another.

Initially Parker promised that none of the music in the movies would be sold on record, but Parker double-crossed Elvis and acted against his client's wishes with an RCA side deal.

Elvis was embarrassed about the movie singles and never thought that they were up to the quality of his other songs. When he learned that they were going to be released for sale, and that his movie scripts were continually getting poorer, he was furious and flatly refused to do any more movies.

Soon, the management relationship took an ugly turn. RCA, plus the entertainment powers behind them, accompanied by Tom Parker, burst into Presley's California mansion for a surprise meeting.

During the meeting it was made forcefully clear to Elvis that they owned him and if he resisted he wouldn't be around to do anything else. In the documentary *Elvis by the Presleys* Jerry Schilling tells of the conversation he had with Elvis over his movie scripts.

Schilling remembered Elvis' comments:

> "Two pictures ago I was a racecar driver, the last picture I was a speed boat racer, this picture they want me to be a motorcycle racer. It's the same script!" Jerry Schilling continues: "He was furious. He didn't go to the studio the next day. This was one of his first times to rebel, and it wasn't long that the studio came up, Colonel came up, and I even think there was somebody from the record company, and bottom line, it was put to Elvis, you will do this and you will do your contracts or you won't do anything."

They weren't threatening Presley's career, they were threatening his life. From the moment Elvis Presley kowtowed to those powers, his life would never again be the same, and in 1964, when the Beatles invaded America, he was already locked into a ridiculous multiyear movie contract that was not in the best interest of his career.

The money continued to flow from the B rate films, which padded the pockets of the hidden powers, but Elvis felt neutered and humiliated. They were prostituting the greatest star in the world for their own personal gain and making him into a laughing stock in the process.

Elvis despised musicals and never wanted to sing in his movies. His true ambition was to develop into a serious dramatic actor and when Barbara Streisand offered him the lead role in A Star is Born, Parker quickly killed the idea.

Parker jacked the price on Elvis appearing in the film up so high that it made his chances of getting the part impossible. Parker had no management experience handling Hollywood actors and he would have lost his meal ticket. He feared that if Elvis went in that direction he would have been out of his element so he found a way to kill the idea. Parker's job was to keep Elvis under his authoritative thumb so RCA and the William Morris agency could keep the gravy train rolling, and roll it did.

With William Morris taking 10% off the top of his musical beach movies, and Parker filling his pockets as well, Elvis' chances of breaking into serious acting were virtually impossible. Just in case anyone thought that Elvis Presley wasn't a great actor, think again; he managed to make everyone believe that he was having a good time making B-rate movies when he was truly in misery.

Photo permission: University of Nevada, Las Vegas Library, Special of Collections

Pictured in this 1960 photograph, taken on the set of *G.I. Blues*, from left to right are Moe Dalitz, Elvis Presley, Juliet Prowse, Wilbur and Toni Clark, Cecil Simmons and Joe Franks (standing behind Wilbur Clark); you'll notice that the only person in the photograph not smiling is Elvis Presley. His somber facial expression exemplifies the pressure that these figureheads, led by Tom Parker, had on his life.

From the late 1950s through the late 1960s, no one had more power in Las Vegas than Moe Dalitz. Morris Barney "Moe" Dalitz ran a leading criminal organization of gangsters called the Cleveland Syndicate, known for its violence and criminal ways while running liquor from Canada and Mexico during prohibition.

In Las Vegas, Dalitz bought The Desert Inn and The Stardust so he could be a "hands-on ally" to Jimmy Hoffa, Meyer Lansky and their entire organized crime network. John L. Smith of the Las Vegas Review-Journal writes of Moe Dalitz:

> *"Early in his life, Dalitz was a bootlegger and racketeer mentioned in the same breath as Meyer Lansky and Benjamin "Bugsy" Siegel. In Cleveland, one longtime member of law enforcement would tell the Kefauver Commission, "Ruthless beatings, unsolved murders and shakedowns, threats and bribery came to this community as a result of gangsters' rise to power."*

Dalitz was the main member of organized crime who helped Frank Sinatra get his big break in show business, and Frank Sinatra was responsible for helping Tom Parker get the motion picture and recording connections that he needed to make Elvis the star that he was.

Knowing the obvious connection between Tom Parker, Frank Sinatra and various other mob members, it should surprise no one that Elvis Presley's co-star in one of his biggest hits of the late 1960's was none other than Nancy Sinatra, Frank Sinatra's daughter.

The added publicity was done as a favor, and although Nancy Sinatra was a very capable actress and co-star, it is doubtful her name would have come up for the role without the stark inside influence. Script after script from 1956 through 1969 would punish Presley's brand as he was commanded to sing sub-par songs that were written by unknown composers.

During those 13 years he suffered through some of the most moronic and repetitive movie plots in the business. This horror started slowly, with Elvis filming one movie a year, but eventually grew to three movies a year until all 31 feature films were completed.

These movies were so low-budget and so rushed to completion that movies like *Girl Happy* and *Spinout* were shot in a mere 30 days. This was an inhuman pace that no entertainer could withstand. Elvis and his Memphis Mafia took to popping pills and staying up for days at a time to meet filming deadlines so Parker's money flow would remain uninterrupted.

On at least one occasion Elvis had a bloody nose that simply wouldn't stop. When the doctor was called to examine him, it was discovered that he was so depleted of sleep brought on by overwork that the nose bleeds wouldn't stop until he got some rest and his resistance could be restored.

Finally, with Elvis on the verge of total physical collapse, Parker's people agreed to give him a few days off. While Elvis and the Memphis Mafia were keeping busy starring in foolish B rate films, Colonel Parker was adding another famous mobster to his book of contacts.

To make the circle of Tom Parker's relationship to the mob complete, enter Las Vegas staple Milton Prell. Prell had been kicking around Las Vegas as long as there was sand in the desert. Prell's first project in Las Vegas, The Bingo Club, was opened in 1947.

In 1952 it was closed for renovation and re-opened as "The Sahara – The Jewel in the Desert." Prell was the front-man for the Detroit mob and it was widely rumored that the money that built the Sahara was bookie, extortion, and west-coast race-wire profits. Parker went out of his way to become close to Prell, showing him the ultimate in respect and consideration.

Alanna Nash clarifies this in her book *The Colonel*, where she writes:

> "The Colonel took a liking to Prell." - "The two formed an intimacy unlike any other in Parker's personal history, and Prell became the one man

the Colonel turned to whenever he needed a favor in Vegas."

The two men were soon joined at the hip, and when Parker learned that Prell's neighbor in Palm Springs was none other than Presley movie producer Hal Wallis, Parker became an eager resident. Palm Springs was also the favorite hangout for Frank Sinatra, his friends in the syndicate, and many Hollywood celebrities of the day.

Milton Prell with Elvis Presley

Parker, becoming totally absorbed in his life of power began to lose his promotional genius, and when Presley's movie career came to an end he was so drunk with power that he has lost his foresight. The radical 60s had taken hold of America and the music scene had become mired in the psychedelic and rock rebellion of the Vietnam era.

There was a new generation afoot that Parker didn't understand. Not because he couldn't, his attention was elsewhere. By 1967, Presley's movie contract was almost complete, and his next career move was uncertain. Elvis turned restless and soon disobedient. He rebelled against Parker and the result was another impromptu meeting and strong lecture.

Parker began to reorganize and take control of everything. He now ran the Memphis Mafia, Elvis' friends and every facet of Elvis' home life. Parker even dictated who Elvis could spend time with, who had to be removed from his inner group and even the types of books he was permitted to read. After Parker ended the meeting where he laid down the law, he pulled Elvis aside and announced that his managerial percentage for handling him was going to be increased to an even 50% / 50% split.

Then, almost as if he were punishing Elvis, he back dated the new contract to the first day of the year. After all, with all of Parker's new pull in the mob, who was going to stop him? No one. Elvis knew that he was outmatched and many of the members in his group were amazed at how quickly he signed the new 50% partnership agreement; Marty Lacker was among them.

After the new contract was signed and the other 25% started to leave the Presley payroll to satisfy Parker's new Mob partner, the two men became obsessed with personal safety. Bars started appearing over the windows and doors of their homes, and they both wired their homes with extensive security systems.

Elvis, who was already a high-degree black belt in karate, started getting his personal bodyguards enrolled in such training and bringing in additional security staff such as Dick Grob, who was a police sergeant, Dave Hebler, who was a martial arts master, and Sam Thompson, a former Shelby County Sheriff Deputy. Around this time, Elvis also went gun crazy, carrying three to five handguns at a time.

Guns became a daily part of his life from this moment on, and they lay strewn all over the house. They could be found lying on sofa cushions, on counters, and even in bathrooms. He also went to great lengths to make sure everyone around him knew that he was highly armed to ward off anyone that wanted to get cute.

He began working martial arts skits in his performances and appearing in photos with his favorite gold-plated revolvers. He went so over-the-edge that as best man at Sonny West's wedding, he'd stand at the altar wearing five loaded firearms, including one in his boot. Elvis was definitely sending a message, but it wasn't being heard.

When Elvis married, Parker arranged every detail as if it were his own wedding. He selected the guests, found the location and even arranged the transportation. The secret location was at the Aladdin Hotel in Las Vegas – a place that Parker knew very well, as it was owned by none other than Milton Prell.

The transportation was also provided by the Mafia. It was Frank Sinatra's private jet. Elvis was in such a cage that he couldn't even plan or enjoy his own wedding without Parker, Sinatra, and Prell calling the shots, just as Eddy Arnold had foreseen and warned Elvis against years earlier.

Parker assembled the wedding, but behind the scenes he never wanted Elvis to marry and did everything to disrupt the couple's happiness. He was good at this: he'd broken up both marriages of both his right-hand men, Tom Diskin and Byron Raphael.

This is covered at length in Alanna Nash's book *The Colonel*. There, Nash explains that Parker kept the men away from home and talked their brides into divorcing them before the ink was dry on their marriage licenses. When the deed was done and he finally got his way, Parker handled every aspect of the divorce.

The Presley marriage went against everything Parker wanted. He felt that the marriage of the No. 1 sex symbol in the world would hurt Presley's sexpot punch from a marketing point of view, and he had secret plans to make Elvis single again – quickly.

After what seemed like a five-minute honeymoon, Parker pushed Elvis apart from his new bride and thrust him into yet another labor-intensive project, the 1968 TV concert. Parker had picked December as the month for the special, and planned it to be a Christmas special, but network producer Steve Binder had other ideas.

After meeting with Elvis for several days and making the ever-sheltered Presley understand that his career was almost shot, Binder realized that this was a great opportunity to re-energize Elvis' career and recapture his raw talent.

The TV special would soon go from Parker's White Christmas to a black leather unplugged concert that reunited Elvis with his old band members. The show was renamed Elvis Presley's "1968 Comeback" and it was an instant success. The deviation from Parker's demands sent him into a rage.

This newcomer had proven himself to be more effective than Parker could have ever been. Parker's advancing age put him out of touch with the popular trends in music and he feared that he was no longer an effective manager.

Parker had always been terrified that one day someone younger would steal his lucrative revenue stream, and Parker saw Steve Binder as this man. He had every reason to be worried: Steve not only got along better with Elvis, he understood the current trends in the music industry, and most importantly, he wasn't afraid of Tom Parker.

After the show was complete, Steve Binder and Elvis Presley parted ways, but not before vowing to remain in contact. They looked forward to many years of friendship, but thanks to Parker not one of Binder's repeated phone calls reached their target.

It would have been the best thing for Presley, but not for Tom Parker. So the friendship, along with all contact, was prevented. Call after call, year after year, was intercepted at Parker's insistence. Immediately after the success Elvis and Binder had enjoyed, Parker put the finishing touches to Presley's marriage by booking him in Las Vegas and keeping Elvis and Priscilla separated.

It was sad, but Elvis and Priscilla never got to enjoy their marriage. Parker did everything possible to keep the newlyweds separate. With a baby girl involved, the strain on the both of them was simply too much for their relationship to bear.

Also thrown into the mix at Parker's request were people surrounding Priscilla filling her head with as much 'women's lib' as possible, designed to transform the subservient young bride into the feminist that Elvis truly despised.

Presley's increased workload, the time away from his wife, his newborn baby, and Pricilla's newfound independence were all manipulated. While performers in today's world would take substantial time off when they're first married to enjoy the moment and raise children, Parker wouldn't allow it.

Taking time off meant no cash flow for Parker, and he had hungry partners. It was supposed to have been the happiest and most enjoyable part of the couple's lives but Parker had other plans.

With the help of his silent *partner* he used his juice to capitalize on the concert success that Steve Binder had orchestrated to negotiate Presley's Las Vegas contract. Rumors widely circulated up and down the Vegas strip that the money that put the deal together came from none other than Milton Prell.

Elvis performed to sellout crowds at the new International Hotel (which later became the Las Vegas Hilton), and he would eventually sign a five-year contract to play one month of solid performances two times a year.

Presley was well paid at $125,000 per week, and he was doing two shows a night (sometimes three) for an hour and fifteen minutes per show, seven days a week. At first, Elvis, Parker and everyone in the Memphis Mafia were having a blast in Sin City. The food, parties, girls, glitz and glamour seemed to be bliss on tap for everyone all the time. Initially, performing in Las Vegas was an exciting new adventure and everyone was treated like royalty.

But by the second and third year the daily grind became exhausting, and Elvis had no breathing room. Alana Nash quotes Lamar Fike*: "Nobody goes to Vegas and plays four weeks anymore – they do five days, tops...and Elvis had such a high energy show that when he would do an honest hour and fifteen minutes twice a night, he was so tired he was cross-eyed."*

While Parker toured every casino in the town, dropping money whenever he put his hand down, Elvis, who was suffering from severe depression, would have to pop even more uppers and downers to keep up with the high demand of his grueling show schedule. The crew was up all night, slept all day, and didn't see sunlight for weeks or even months at a time.

Everyone had seen enough of Las Vegas, especially Elvis, who was bored to tears with the same songs, and repetition. It was the same show day in and day out, but Parker wouldn't allow any variations because he was making money.

To get his point across, Elvis would intentionally do lackluster shows just to piss the old man off. He would sing lying on his back on stage, do karate exhibitions and even talk with the audience instead of perform. He thought surely this would wake Parker up, but he didn't care because the money was flowing.

By the last year of the contract Presley was in total torment and it became very clear that the only thing Tom Parker cared about was the flashing lights and the excitement of the tables. Exactly how bad was Parker's gambling habit? This is best explained by two members of Presley's entourage in the documentary *Elvis: The Last 24 Hours*. Lamar Fike explains:

> "Colonel Parker was probably one of the most degenerate gamblers I have ever known in my life. In Nevada they used to say his money wasn't worth anything. In a period of an hour and a half he lost over a million and a quarter."

In the same DVD, Larry Geller, another of Presley's close friends, recalls a time when he was walking through the casino and saw a crowd of people around a man gambling. As he drew closer, he saw that the area was roped off and the man gambling and creating such a stir was Tom Parker.

Parker spotted Larry and asked him to sit by him for good luck. Larry explains what he saw: *"The Colonel was there for hours* (playing the wheel of fortune game with stacks of chips)*, upon hours until 5 o'clock in the morning, and he lost one and a half million dollars that night."*

According to the National Average Wage Index, the average wage in 1969 was $5,893.76, and Parker was gambling away millions of dollars without batting an eye. Parker was totally out of control and had lost sight of his fiduciary responsibly to his client. He also thought his job was done: Elvis was booked, and now the shows were up to Elvis. Unfortunately, the talent that Parker had for promotional skill, he lacked in humanity and human compassion.

Tickets to Elvis' shows were very inexpensive at a mere $40. That price included the ticket to the show and a gourmet meal. Anyone in Las Vegas would have easily paid double, as Elvis was the hottest ticket in town. After a time it appeared obvious that Parker was "giving Elvis away" just to be close to the gambling tables. Parker had Elvis' career on auto-pilot but the world was changing.

1969 was a pivotal year in America. Long gone were the crew cuts and miniskirts of the 1950's conservative America. The youth of the day had been hijacked by drugs, disobedience, sexual promiscuity, long, greasy hair and a thirst for psychedelic music. In August of that year the Woodstock Music Festival was held at a dairy farm in a small town in the lower region of New York State.

This venue attracted the best musical acts in America, and Elvis wasn't invited. In fact, he wasn't even thought of. Instead, the audience of more than 400,000 saw Jimi Hendrix, The Who, The Band, Janis Joplin, Johnny Winter, Creedence Clearwater Revival, Jefferson Airplane, Ten Years After, Joan Baez, Santana, Joe Cocker, and a band named Crosby, Stills, Nash, and Young.

While Elvis was still playing to sellout crowds, and was making a small fortune doing it, he began to notice that the age group of his audience was changing. He was still drawing young people but they were fewer than that had been in the past. Searching for answers to what he was seeing he began watching more news broadcasts and he soon learned how out of touch he was with the American youth.

What he saw was frightening. The Vietnam War was escalating, which tested the patriotism of American citizens and protesting youth were burning the American flag. Meanwhile, John Lennon was having huge anti-war protests which were drawing thousands of people, and he was giving the Nixon administration fits.

Because of Lennon's protests, draft cards were being burned as young Americans were ignoring their countries call to duty. This negatively impacted what the military could do. With manpower being stretched thin in Vietnam, the result was hundreds, if not thousands, of unnecessary American casualties that were far beyond expectation. This fueled the outrage and increased the number of protests, and so the vicious cycle continued.

Needless to say, Lennon was not a fan of the American government, and the feeling was mutual. To Nixon, Lennon was many things; he was a national security threat and a social nuisance, but whatever he was, he was not an American citizen.

Because he was a foreigner who was hijacking the country's population away from their Government's desired path, he silently climbed to the top of the FBI's hit list. Soon the FBI began to monitor his every move and record his every word. In no time Lennon's FBI file grew into the thousands of pages.

The White House knew that something had to be done. At the same time, Elvis had many things going through his head, and all roads went through Washington DC. Elvis was the polar opposite of Lennon. He hated illegal drugs, he was fiercely patriotic, and didn't like the radical uproar that he saw in America. To Presley, it was a personal call to arms.

On December 19th 1970 Elvis was on a commercial airplane when he found himself seated next to a politician. The two began talking and about the problems facing the nation and with little encouragement Elvis began writing a letter to President Nixon.

In the letter he explained that he was very eager to help the US Government take down the illegal drug culture. This is a typed version of his letter which I acquired copyright-free at the National Archives. The first sentence of the last paragraph states *"I am glad to help just so long as it is kept very private"*.

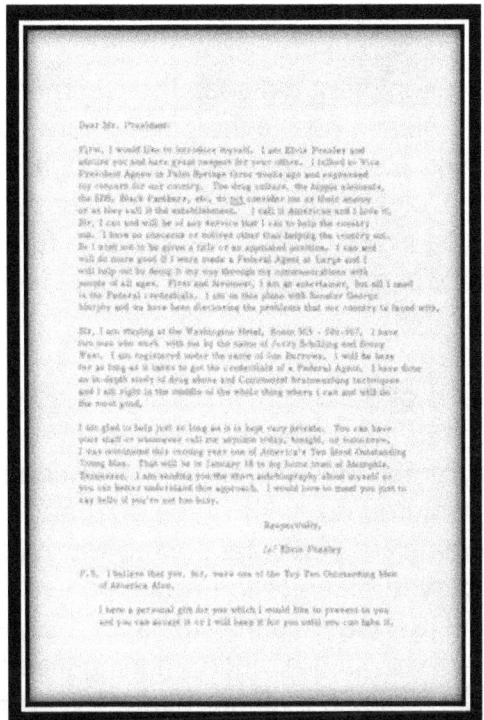

Two days later Elvis met President Nixon in a private meeting in the Oval Office. While behind closed doors he outlined his concerns regarding the anti-American sentiment that he believed came from John Lennon. Elvis offered his help and the two men were in total agreement.

When Elvis returned home and made the announcement of his new federal credentials, Parker and the mobsters behind him had a very big problem. With his newfound federal powers, which gave him a sense of confidence against Parker and his thugs, Elvis decided the time was right to dump Tom Parker once and for all. If he'd said it once, he'd said it a thousand times: *"I hate that old man, and I'm tired of the old bastard threatening me"*.

The resentment between the two men had festered and blossomed to the point where almost anything could produce a screaming match. Elvis, tired of being the Colonel's puppet, fumed over the lack of control he had in his career. He was also furious over the lack of a worldwide tour that Parker said years ago was in the works.

Millions of dollars in offers continued to pour in from all parts of the globe, including an offer to play at the great pyramids of Giza. All would go unanswered as Parker conjured up one excuse after another. One screaming match in particular started when Elvis heard that an employee of the Hilton was fired while his wife was sick and just diagnosed with cancer. Elvis blew his stack on stage about the matter, hurling insults at Barron Hilton, president of the Hilton Hotel chain.

This was a direct and public insult to a mob friendly hotel. A hush sprawled over the audience as they listened to what Elvis had to say. After the show Parker was purple with rage when he appeared in Presley's dressing room and the two men went 'nose to nose'. The tirade continued upstairs in Presley's thirteenth-floor suite. Finally, after Parker pounded the floor with his cane for nearly an hour, Elvis did what he'd been threatening to do for years: he fired him.

The next day Parker produced a bill with itemized expenses for Elvis to buy him out of his contract. The bill was for millions of dollars that Elvis simply didn't have and Parker knew it. Elvis was stuck. As the two men grinded their axes bigger troubles were on the horizon.

Unbeknownst to President Nixon, a Mafia leak from within the White House sought to alert his cronies from coast to coast that Elvis had obtained federal law enforcement credentials and was no longer to be trusted. The informer quietly contacted her media outlets, and the secrecy that Presley demanded in his letter to President Nixon was blown.

Now everyone from Texas to Transylvania knew what Elvis was up to, and he lost the trust of not only his fellow stars, but also the people who were partnering with his manager. The Washington Post published the following information for all eyes to see. The following article was acquired copyright-free at the National Archives:

    From the moment this article hit the press Elvis Presley was no longer seen as an entertainer. He was a marked man. This unforeseen media event devastated Presley, and put him at great risk, but paled in comparison to what followed in his personal life.

    Back at home Priscilla was succumbing to the pressures of life alone, and she was no longer satisfied with the time apart from her husband. The long and secret affair she was having with Elvis' friend and karate instructor would be exposed and would prove to be the ultimate insult. Priscilla was much more than just a wife for Elvis; she was a very important part of his mental makeup.

She was the one person he poured his guts out to when his mother died, and she became the ultimate confidant and transitional object. In her, Elvis finally had someone whom he could completely and thoroughly trust, but when that ended, his world totally collapsed.

In August of 1972, they filed for divorce, and Tom Parker finally got what he wanted all along. Elvis was single again. He managed to contort Elvis' marriage into ruin, but Parker now had to deal with a bigger problem.

Elvis, to ease the pain of losing Priscilla, turned to abusing his prescription medicines. Elvis' new found drug use would prove to be a far bigger nuisance for Parker than his marriage ever was.

As Parker tried to put Elvis back together again, Presley's lawyer worked out the amicable terms of the settlement. Priscilla would receive $100,000 in a lump sum, plus $1,000 monthly for expenses and $500 monthly for child support. Each went their separate ways, and the divorce was finalized.

Some people take drugs to escape physical pain, Elvis took drugs to escape mental pain, and as 1972 turned into 1973 there was plenty of mental anguish to go around. Elvis was on the brink of financial collapse, his wife had left him and was living with one of his friends, the whole world knew that he was a federal narc, and his creativity was being stifled by his manager. There was no way out.

The stormy relationship between Presley and Parker continued as Presley's drug use escalated. Trying to satisfy the numerous requests and offers from around the globe for Elvis to do a worldwide tour, Parker set up a television broadcast via satellite and arranged to have it pumped into every country.

The show, *Aloha from Hawaii*, was to air on January 14, 1973 and was the world's first live-concert satellite broadcast, reaching two billion viewers. To prepare for this major event, Presley dieted down to a mere 175 pounds and stayed off his medication for weeks.

He also designed the now-famous jeweled eagle motif for the jumpsuit that he wore. The double album that was created from this show would stay on the charts for 36 weeks and would prove to be his first chart-topping LP in nearly a decade.

By February it was selling over a million copies in the US alone, and far more in foreign countries, but sadly, it would prove to be his last and final moment as a glorious superstar – it would be his last No. 1 album.

As 1973 wore on, Presley and Parker continued to battle. They fought over Elvis' insistence to record his music in Memphis and the new gospel group that Elvis had just signed on for $100,000.

Parker was furious, and remixed Presley's songs, not releasing the version that Presley had produced himself. This was discovered as Elvis was riding in a car with Jerry Schilling and his new song was announced for the first time on the radio, and the version played was nothing Elvis had heard before.

The suppression of creativity that no one understood, combined with the business end of entertainment that he had no say in, put Elvis into deep depression. In the end, both Presley and Parker had succumbed to their compulsions.

Parker wanted desperately to return to the green felt of the casinos but needed to pay off his gambling marker that Hal Wallis, RCA and the Hilton were still holding, and Presley needed to get over this financial hump and go back to losing money the old-fashioned way – by paying for all the expenses and splitting the remainder with Parker.

Later that year, Elvis' ex-wife reopened the divorce settlement, claiming that she'd settled for far too little. This time around she'd receive $725,000 in cash, $4,200 a month spousal support for a year (which had ballooned to $6,000 a month for a total of ten years), along with $4,000 in monthly child support.

Added to this, she'd also receive 5% of Elvis' publishing companies and half of their house in California. Elvis, now with his finances in shambles and in desperate need of a cash injection, doubled his work schedule. Soon Parker told Elvis that he had a way for him to net a quick $4.5 million.

He coaxed Elvis to sell his music royalties for a lump sum of cash to RCA. With both men needing a financial shot in the arm, the Colonel made the deal. Parker's longtime friends at RCA quickly signed the sweet deal that got Parker off the hook for his gambling debts and Elvis off the hook for the money he owed his ex-wife.

It should have been a great deal for everyone involved but it wasn't. This was possibly the worst business deal ever concocted in music history. The two men got $10.5 million in total, and under their new 50/50 split, Elvis got $4.5 million before taxes.

After the taxman and his ex-wife took their chunk almost nothing remained. Literally everyone gained something in this deal but Presley. RCA got profits, Parker settled his gambling debts, Priscilla went on her merry way and Elvis got the shaft.

The lump-sum payment was far too cheap for possibly the most valuable recordings in of the history of popular music. It became clear that this wasn't a contract - this was a robbery. An official investigation after Elvis' death discovered that *"both Colonel Parker and RCA acted in collusion against Presley's best interests. Colonel Parker was guilty of self-dealing and overreaching and had violated his duty to both Elvis and to the estate."*

This quote originated from official estate documents. It serves as proof positive that Colonel Parker took advantage of a financially desperate and emotionally drained man to fill his own pockets.

www.TCB-World.com contains the following quotes regarding the RCA deal in March of 1973:

"Jack Soden of EPE (Elvis Presley Enterprises) describes the deal as being right up there with the Indians selling Manhattan for $24. Seven years later, a lawyer for the Presley Estate, Blanchard Tual, concluded that Colonel Parker and RCA were probably guilty of collusion, conspiracy, fraud and misrepresentation."

As the year progressed, so did the tension and at the end of the summer session in Las Vegas, Elvis and Parker were red-faced and nose-to-nose again. Elvis ended the final show of his tour with the words *"To Hell with the Hilton Hotel,"* and Elvis met Parker backstage for a showdown in front of his entire entourage.

This time Elvis put it in point-blank terms: *"I don't want to play here anymore. You son-of-a-bitch, don't book me here again!"* Parker fired back with *"I'm the manager and I'll book you where I see fit!"* Elvis was tired of Las Vegas and tired of Parker. *"You can gamble in Las Vegas on another singer's dime – you're fired!"* Elvis then publicly named Concert West manager Tom Hulett, Led Zeppelin's manager, as Parker's replacement.

Bending to Presley's demands, the Colonel joined the rest of the entertainment world and started booking concerts in city arenas. Elvis and crew would play 100 towns a year, which was an inhuman workload which bordered on entertainment servitude.

His grueling tour schedule would regularly include gigs in a different town each night, covering 200 or 300 miles between concert locations at breakneck speed. As Presley's music grew more diverse and operatic, his band and supporting crew also grew.

Nearly 100 people, including a backing vocal group, soloists, an entire orchestra, two planes and many buses were now part of Presley's stage show. With his monstrous and expanding payroll, the lack of tax shelters, no more royalties from his songs, and a 50% split with Colonel Parker of everything he made, Elvis had to work himself into total exhaustion just to keep his financial head above water.

Although he continued to play to sellout crowds and made an astounding wage, he was always one tour away from a financial meltdown. As Elvis slipped deeper into his own universe of depression, financial ruin, and exhaustion, he avoided Parker at every turn using buffers – typically Joe Esposito – to communicate his will.

In 1975, as Elvis' 40th birthday approached, he remained secluded at his Graceland compound complete with armed guards, soundproof walls and wrought-iron fences between himself and the outside world. Fueling his malaise were magazines that ran cover stories about Presley's 40th birthday showing unflattering photos of the man with captions like "Elvis: fat and forty". To Elvis, who privately suffered from low self-esteem and was riddled with self-doubt, this caused a catastrophic meltdown.

By 1976, Elvis was pushed to the very breaking point resulting in exhaustion and hospitalization. Larry Geller was on tour with Elvis in Louisville, Kentucky, witnessing the horror that had become Presley's life. He sums the situation up in *Elvis: The Last 24 hours"*

> "Dr. Nick was holding Elvis' head, Elvis was in the bed, semi-conscious, almost comatose and he was moaning and he was in such bad shape and Dr. Nick was dunking Elvis's head into a bucket of ice water to revive him –[Colonel Parker Entered]- the door closed, and I thought immediately: Okay, this is good, this is good, now the old man, Parker, is going to see what's going on here, and he's going to see the bad shape Elvis is in and he's going to do something about it. I mean you can't allow this to go on, it's inhuman! Ninety seconds later the door opened up, Colonel Parker walks up to me and I get up and we stand toe to toe, and he stares coldly into my eyes and says: 'Now you listen to me; the only thing that's important is that that man is on stage tonight – nothing else matters – nothing.'"

Elvis was unaware that Colonel Parker was trying to sell his contract, and during the private negotiation someone leaked the story to a Tennessee newspaper named the Nashville Banner. In their article they claimed that a group of businessmen had expressed interest in the purchase and that negotiations were ongoing.

The article continued to quote sources from both Memphis and Los Angeles and the news shocked the country. Suddenly everyone was put on high alert that there were major problems brewing between Elvis and Parker.

Although Parker's financial desperation was mounting, the negotiations were unsuccessful, and the two sides couldn't come to terms. As the relationship with Parker deteriorated by the day, the Memphis Mafia was rotting from within. Suddenly everyone seemed to have a bone to pick with their employer for one reason or another.

Joe Esposito and a group of investors wanted money from Elvis to open a chain of Racquet Ball Courts. The venture went bankrupt leaving the two men and their investors hostile toward each other.

Presley's personal physician, Dr. George Nichopoulos, borrowed money from Presley to build a gigantic office complex in Memphis. That venture also went bust leaving Dr. Nick unable to repay Presley which created friction.

David Stanley, one of Presley's step brothers, was in the middle of a divorce and claimed that Elvis was the problem with their marriage. Shortly thereafter, three of Elvis' body guards: Red West, Sonny West and Dave Hebler, had to be let go due to financial reasons with little notice, and they all swore revenge.

Presley's girlfriend, Ginger Alden, who was both immature and headstrong, needed to have everything her way, and the couple seemed to battle endlessly. She had also developed a fondness for David Stanley, who had an axe to grind with Elvis due to his failing marriage. Suddenly everyone was driving Elvis to the brink of frustration and depression.

In early April of 1977 Elvis was still battling with his manager, and almost his entire inner circle of employees and friends. He was eventually hospitalized with exhaustion and a few shows had to be cancelled. Naturally, Tom Parker, who had more interest in his paycheck then he did in Elvis, was furious.

Parker, who was stalling for time to repay his gambling debts, focused on the public announcement for the CBS-TV special entitled *Elvis in Concert*. This was to be Elvis' last concert on last leg of his tour. The concert date was set for June 26, 1977 and the location was a brand new facility in Indianapolis named Market Square Arena.

The concert was a great performance for a man who was sick, medicated and near total exhaustion. Finally the checks were banked and everyone returned home for some much needed rest and relaxation. No one had any idea that Elvis would never live long enough to see the concert televised. During his tour break from June 27th through August 15th, Elvis remained in seclusion.

All he wanted to do was relax, spend some time with his 9-year-old daughter, and unwind in his favorite place on earth, the upstairs at Graceland. Much like Superman's "Fortress of Solitude," Graceland's upstairs was Presley's ultimate sanctuary away from the world.

There he could rest, watch TV, read, or just simply enjoy his privacy, and if he needed anything he could simply call downstairs where his maid or personal valet would attend to his every desire.

Another feature of Graceland's upstairs that greatly appealed to Elvis were the blacked-out windows and special-tufted foam padding that were installed to soundproof his bedroom suite as well as the whole second floor.

This special soundproofing came in very handy as Vernon and his second wife, Dee Stanley, were fighting daily and ready to separate. Vernon, knowing that Elvis was involved with undercover operations for the government, and knowing that a divorce from Dee was inevitable, advised his son to have his will changed.

"My God, if anything happened to you Dee and her boys would get millions. This can't happen son, we're splitting up. That will has to be changed." Doing as he was told Elvis visited his attorney and adjusted his last will and testament removing Dee and her three boys. This created a houseful of bad feelings as Graceland erupted.

By mid-July it became obvious that his three fired body guards made good on their promise to get revenge by publishing dirt on Elvis and his behind-the-scenes exploits.

Portions of their 'tell-all' book began to surface in some foreign countries, as well as through several news conferences that announced snippets of its content as well as their venomous motivation for the writing it.

The highly sensationalized (if not totally fabricated) tales within the childish publication were designed to ruin Elvis' career. The book was published in America on August 4th, and was entitled "Elvis: What Happened?"

Elvis read the book with tears pouring down his face. *"I bought them everything, from gold rings, to new Cadillacs. How could they do this to me?!"* He was heartbroken and stunned at the betrayal. Rocked to his core he was battling middle age, bankruptcy, depression, numerous health problems and a growing prescription drug problem.

Parker slowly came to the realization he just lost any chance he had of selling Presley's contract. Suddenly there was enough aggression between Elvis Presley, his manager, his employees, Vernon's ex-wife, his girlfriend, the mob, his step-brothers, and his three former bodyguards to murder a herd of cattle. All of them had an axe to grind for one reason or another, but only one of them wanted him dead.

2
The Discovery

"Then Warlick tried to explain the importance of the clues he had found at the death scene, the medical examiner cut him off"

- The Death of Elvis-

Monday, August 15th 1977, a steamy day in Memphis – a day typical of the humid summers that Tennesseans have learned to bear. The sun rose as peacefully that morning as it had in ordinary fashion since the murder of Dr. Martin Luther King Jr., 9 years prior.

By 7:00am., the thick mist of the morning dew burned off the foliage and created a fog in the air so thick that it hung, draped and suspended, for hours. As the city woke and its citizens hustled about their daily routines, no one had the slightest clue that at nearby Graceland, Elvis Presley would be spending his final day on earth.

The world would little notice, nor long remember this morning, but in the 24 hours that followed, the city of Memphis, as well as the far reaches of the globe, would be forever changed. This day started like any other before Elvis embarked on a new tour. Tom Parker, Lamar Fike, and numerous other personal aides and employees had boarded a 747 to fly out of town.

Their purpose was to prepare the concert destination for Presley's arrival the following day. When they arrived in Portland, Maine, Presley's setup crew – or 24-hour crew, as they are known in the circus industry – would prepare the stage and lighting, handle the security detail, set up the merchandising and secure the entire floor where Elvis would stay.

As trustworthy as they were busy, the setup crew knew exactly what to do. As the swarm of people hustled to complete their duties in Portland, the bustle back at Graceland was just beginning. By 8:00 a.m., the few remaining security staffers had left Graceland along with Presley's personal valet. They had left for the day and those who replaced them were readying equipment for the upcoming tour.

Joe Esposito, Presley's group foreman and road manager, had flown in from his home in California to oversee the process and make the necessary arrangements for a timely departure. It was the usual pre-tour fuss that everyone had experienced a thousand times before. Joe was a key employee with many responsibilities and there was no one better for the job.

Presley staffer, Al Strada, was charged with a key responsibility: locate and carefully pack all of Presley's wardrobe and other personal effects, while longtime friend, Graceland resident and stage manager, Charlie Hodge, frantically coordinated his end of the fray. It was his responsibility to pack Presley's stage gear.

On this morning, they faced an all-too-common predicament as they were slightly behind schedule. The men were working hand-in-hand with every interval step being reported to Joe Esposito, who was being remotely controlled by Tom Parker in Portland. Elvis and the rest of the men at Graceland were scheduled to depart for Portland at 4:00 p.m. to join their setup crew.

The break between the tour legs was over and everyone groaned at the thought of going back to work because it was such an enormous undertaking. Long gone were the days of Elvis grabbing his guitar and a few buddies and driving to the next gig. By 1977 Presley's equipment and tour personnel tour had now grown to enormous proportions. Fortunately, for everyone, this was the last tour leg of the year.

The years had worn on Presley as well as his entourage. Gone were the vibrant smiles and carefree days. There were no more pranks played by mischievous lads, practical jokes, or bursts of laughter behind the scenes. By 1977, those lads were now 40-something and had either left the Memphis Mafia entirely, or had been replaced by pudgy, middle-aged caricatures of their former selves, whose hard life on the road had worn heavily on both their bodies and their minds.

The spark of youth and excitement had long since faded, and the tomfoolery of their twenties was all but a memory. The adventure of life on the road, celebrity parties and droves of women had given way to a mundane existence and the rigors of routine.

As middle age hit the group, the Presley staffers entered a whole new phase of life – no longer fun or carefree, but rife with divorce, prescription-drug abuse, and overindulgence.

The fun the group once enjoyed in abundance had collapsed into the daily bickering of grown men who wrestled with the reality of not only their lost youth, but their lost identities. By August of 1977 there was tension, responsibility, and even hard feelings among the group.

The events of Elvis Presley's final hours were established through the undertaking of countless hours of interviewing his employees and family members as well as the use of private investigators.

The general consensus of those combined investigations produced the following results that have been printed, reprinted, and repeated seemingly millions of times in books, websites, and magazines around the world.

The much repeated story begins as August 15th fades into night. Elvis was in need of some minor dental work prior to the start of his tour. At 10:00 p.m. Elvis, accompanied by Ginger Alden and his nine year old daughter, Lisa Marie, leave Graceland.

Elvis was driving his favorite car, a black 1973 Stutz Blackhawk III, with Ginger in the passenger seat and his daughter seated in the rear. Such visits were not uncommon at this hour due to Elvis' nocturnal existence. The trio arrived at Dr. Hoffman's office for his 10:30 p.m. appointment, returning to Graceland's gates just after midnight. As Elvis entered Graceland, he greeted numerous members of his staff as some had just flown into town to ready for the upcoming tour. After a few minutes of chat with his friends Elvis and Ginger escaped upstairs to his private quarters. It was Tuesday 12:43am on the 16th of August, and it would be the last time they would ever see Elvis Presley alive.

4:00 am - A mere twelve hours before Elvis was slated to fly out of town and begin his tour, he phoned his cousin Billy Smith (Who had, along with his wife, a house on Graceland's sprawling lot) to arrange a game of doubles in racquetball between Elvis, Ginger, Billy and his wife Jo.

It is reported that Elvis was still wearing his DEA jogging suit that he'd worn to the dentist. According to his cousin Billy, during the game Elvis had whacked himself on the shin with his racquet hard enough to leave a welt. According to Billy, Presley's injury was sufficient enough to end the game.

6:00 am - After the racquetball games had ended, Elvis sat at the piano in the lounge area of the racquetball building and played songs to entertain Ginger, Billy, and Jo for approximately 20 minutes. After their musical interlude, Elvis and Ginger retired to the upstairs suite where Billy Smith claims to have followed them to wash and dry Elvis' hair. Afterward, Smith returned to his home and Elvis changed into his pajamas, watched TV, and began to read.

8:30 am - Elvis, unable to sleep, calls Dr. Nichopolous at his office, asking his nurse for sleeping pills. Nurse Tish Henley begins to relay two sleeping pills to Elvis through her husband. These pills were received at Graceland by Elvis' Aunt, Delta Mae, and found their way upstairs to Elvis through his personal valet.

9:30 am - Ginger Alden alleges that Elvis, still restless, got out of bed and walked into the bathroom to read carrying a book. She further alleges that she warned him not to fall asleep while reading in the bathroom. According to Ginger he looked back at her, smiled, and replied *"Don't worry, I won't."*

2:34 pm - Ginger Alden wakes up and discovers Elvis' body on the bathroom floor. She panics and uses the intercom to call for help. The intercom rang in the kitchen and was handed to Al Strada. Strada runs up the stairs to help. Moments later, he returns downstairs in a panic to find Joe Esposito. Esposito is quickly located, climbs the stairs and begins CPR in an effort to revive Presley.

Esposito then calls Dr. Nichopolous and then the Fire Department Rescue squad. Ten minutes later EMTs arrive and continue CPR attempts despite both rigor-mortis and livor mortis being present (rigor-mortis is the stiffening of the body and skin, and livor mortis is the skin turning purple/black in color caused by blood pooling in the body as the heart is no longer circulating it).

2:52 pm - Dr. Nichopolous arrives just as the body was being loaded into the ambulance. There, he climbs onboard joining Joe Esposito and Charlie Hodge. In the back of the vehicle the men frantically assist Dr. Nichopolous who continues to work on Presley in an attempt to revive him. Their destination is the emergency room at Baptist Memorial Hospital.

Upon their arrival at Baptist Memorial, the emergency medical "Harvey Team" is called and quickly responds. At the same time, Elvis' personal nurse, Marian Cocke, is paged. She is astonished when she answers the page to learn that the "Harvey Team" is being called to work on Elvis.

3:09 p.m. - Marian Cocke quickly arrives in the emergency room and meets Charlie Hodge. Hodge explains to her that the situation looks grave. After consoling Hodge, Cocke enters to the trauma room joining Dr. Nichopolous as well as the other members of the "Harvey Team."

3:12 p.m. - Marian Cocke witnesses both heroic and horrific lifesaving attempts. Knowing by his appearance that Elvis has long been dead, Cocke calls off further procedures. Emergency lifesaving efforts cease, and Elvis Presley is pronounced dead.

The assembly of family members and entourage at the Hospital are notified by Dr. Nichopolous, and Esposito begins making phone calls – first to Tom Parker and immediately afterward to Priscilla.

3:15 p.m. - A member of the Baptist Memorial Hospital staff asks Esposito if he would like to make the announcement to the media. Joe was then stopped by Dr. Nichopolous from making any announcements until Vernon Presley was told face to face. This was a wise move, as Vernon was not in good health and this phone call would be devastating. Fifteen minutes later, Vernon is notified in person at Graceland.

3:34 p.m. - A spokesperson for Baptist Memorial Hospital informs the media that Elvis has died. The shock spreads worldwide, and radio stations from Germany to Brazil interrupt programming to play continuous Elvis hits. Pandemonium breaks out at Baptist Memorial Hospital as well as at Graceland. The city of Memphis is in turmoil.

From the minute Elvis was declared dead and prepped for autopsy, the remaining members of Presley's entourage began finding their way back to Graceland. In *The Day Elvis Presley Died*, Joe Esposito explains:

> "Charlie and Billy and I all hugged each other and had the police department...one of the police-department men took us back to the house. Graceland, just went into a mode to help."

When the men arrived back at Graceland, they witnessed a hysterical beehive of activity. The comings and goings of family, employees and friends, coupled with police officers left behind to secure the death scene had made it almost impossible to monitor the activity, and no one did.

As EMTs Ulysses Jones and Charles Crosby returned from the hospital to retrieve the medical equipment that they had left behind at the death scene, they immediately knew something was wrong. They were shocked to discover that the entire area had been completely sanitized, and their equipment had been gathered and neatly condensed into a tidy pile in the far corner of the room.

They knew this was not how the scene was left, and it became obvious that someone had cleaned. Ulysses Jones, in the book *The Death of Elvis* explains this further: *"Everything was cleaned up. The bed had been made, the restroom and everything had been cleaned up. The papers were all gone."* The EMTs were puzzled and began to ponder what had happened.

After all, why did the Memphis Police bother leaving officers at Graceland to guard the upstairs and charge them with the responsibility of preserving the death scene for an investigation when the death scene was tampered with? Surely the police knew through their training that this would negate any investigation into the death.

So, ask the questions. The ones you're already thinking. If the police didn't allow anyone to enter – did they clean the room? Who gave the order? Why? After a few minutes of head scratching, the EMTs walked down the stairs with their resuscitation equipment and readied themselves for their next emergency call. For them, this nightmare had ended.

On their way out of Graceland, they passed investigator Dan Warlick, Lt. McCachren, and Assistant District Attorney Jerry Stauffer entering the foyer. They marched intently up the stairs to the death scene with stern faces. Immediately after Elvis had been declared dead, the men had assembled themselves and came to Graceland armed with an "insta-matic" camera, pens and notepads.

Jones and Crosby knew the men were in search of answers and they knew that they wouldn't find any. They also knew that the newly sanitized room they were about to discover was not going to make them very happy, and indeed it did not.

As the decades rolled past, Jones and Crosby would mull over these odd happenings endlessly in search of answers as the cause of Presley's death became more and more in question.

They both knew the gravity of a hastily sanitized death scene but couldn't understand why it was done, or who allowed it. Eventually both men would go to their graves without answers.

What Dan Warlick and his men would find upon entering the upstairs is covered in Thompson and Cole's classic book *The Death of Elvis*. They write:

"Down the hall Warlick recognized a beefy, red-faced man with white hair. It was Vernon Presley. He seemed composed. "My baby is

dead," Warlick heard Vernon say into the telephone. "They've taken him. He's gone. My baby has died."

Then Vernon burst out crying and was overcome by such uncontrolled spasms of grief that it nearly buckled him in two. The men puzzled momentarily at what had just come out of Vernon Presley's mouth – what did Vernon mean by *"they?"* They - meaning more than one? What could that possibly mean? The investigators looked at each other momentarily and continued up the stairs to the death scene.

Thompson and Cole's *The Death of Elvis* continues: *"(Sam) Thompson lead Warlick, McCachren, Peel, Millian and Stauffer up the staircase to a second-floor hallway. Thompson had stopped twice to unlock a couple of doors sealing off Elvis' bedroom suite."*

It was there, in Elvis' office, that Dan Warlick discovered his first clue, almost as if it jumped out and grabbed him. Placed in plain view on Elvis' desk was an empty syringe. It was placed so perfectly on the desk place that it looked like there were arrows pointing to it. It was simply impossible to miss.

Warlick thought that the placement of the syringe was odd, but upon further inspection this discovery became baffling. Not only was the syringe empty but it had no needle. The men were speechless and looked at each other in disbelief. Elvis had syringes lying around? Why? Why this type of syringe? Where's the needle? Why was it missing? Where did it go?

When I spoke to Dan about the syringe in our meeting in Nashville, Tennessee, on November 3rd of 2017, he described how odd the syringe was. *"It wasn't an ordinary syringe that you would imagine. It was a cartridge type of syringe. I don't know if that's the proper term or not but that's what I call them. It was the kind that was designed to hold a cartridge of medicine held in place by a steel frame."*

After a few minutes of careful examination, the men pressed onward. They rounded the corner and walked into Elvis Presley's bedroom. It was a room that millions of women wanted to get into, but it was possibly one of the most secluded and private rooms in the country.

Elvis' inner sanctum was decorated in black padded leather with red velvet curtains and it had a red velvet valance on the ceilings perimeter. The curtains and tie backs were ornately trimmed with short gold fringe. The velvet draperies and shag red carpeting provided a luxurious backdrop for the religious statue that stood watch over the bed. It was truly a bedroom fit for a king.

The walls behind the head of the bed and at the opposite side of the room were clad with full length mirrors. Behind the bed the mirrors stretched from corner to corner, and on a wall opposite the room the mirror ended where the blacked out windows began.

Ten feet off the foot of the bed was a three-foot-long ceramic tiger that had been placed on top of a 27-inch console television set. The television cabinet was large and had wide speakers on each side of the screen. Its custom-made stand raised the screen just high enough to be visible from the comfort of Elvis' pillow.

Graceland's decor has long since been dwarfed by modern day wealth and technology, but in the late 1970s it was a marvel of comfort, class, and elegance that few others could have imagined, let alone enjoyed. It was truly a feast for the eyes as the investigators scanned the room for clues.

To the left of the television set, the investigators saw a large bookcase that housed several smaller television sets. These monitors were part of Elvis' closed circuit security system. This very expensive and 'state of the art' system allowed Elvis to monitor Graceland's entire grounds from the comfort of his eight foot wide bed.

As the men walked closer, they noticed a shiny chrome pistol against the black and red backdrop of the bedroom. It was on top of an armoire. They felt the metal to see if it had been recently fired, but it was stone cold.

The allure of the surroundings soon gave way to the shock that they felt when they discovered the number of guns Presley had in his collection. In plain view was an arsenal of pistols, M16s, and even fully automatic machine guns. Amazingly, these weapons were casually strewn in every room as if they were ashtrays.

As they investigated further, they found another syringe. This syringe was also located in plain view on top of the bookshelf and below the security system monitors. It was at eye level toward the front edge of the bookshelf.

It was as impossible to miss as the last syringe. After further inspection it was also empty and missing its needle. The men stopped for several minutes to examine the syringe they had found being careful not to touch anything. After the wide eyed visual scrutiny subsided, they looked at each other in total disbelief.

How do you digest and process such things? Automatic weapons? Pistols? Empty syringes with no needles? Stuffed teddy bears lining the walls of Presley's office? Blacked out windows? Thick tufted black leather padding to soundproof the room? It was all too much for these investigators, or any investigators, to digest. The men were experiencing an overload of the senses, and there wasn't anyone in the world that could have blamed them.

Investigator Dan Warlick's feelings on his eyewitness accounts are fully covered in *The Death of Elvis*.

"'I'll tell you, those two injectable syringes really made me wonder what in the world was going on here.'" Then Warlick came upon a discovery that made him furious. "'The bed's been made up,' he exclaimed. 'It shouldn't have been made. Somebody has cleaned up the place.' Stauffer watched Warlick's anger boil . . . "

As Warlick's blood pressure soared, a very nervous Joe Esposito rushed up the stairs to relieve Sam Thompson, a member of Elvis' security team, of his tour guide duties. Esposito had just gotten off the phone with Tom Parker in Portland, Maine, where he had received quick instructions to join the investigation team and take over as host.

When Esposito arrived they had already turned to the right and proceeded through the doorway to Presley's bathroom. There they found more eye popping objects that baffled their reasoning. This was no ordinary bathroom. It was a bathroom, a reading lounge, a dressing room, and a wardrobe area all rolled into one. This was Elvis' favorite room in the house.

There the soundproofing and solitude allowed him the privacy he needed to read his many books and have private talks with anyone he wanted. Its deep shag carpeting gave the room a very comfortable feel. It was a casual room for casual purposes, but no one dared to enter unless they were invited. It was strictly and completely off-limits.

The men stood in the doorway facing the dressing and wardrobe area directly across the room. They later learned that the area was originally designed for a personal bodyguard to have a bed as well as other accommodations, but it was not to be.

Why it was necessary to have a body guard that close to Elvis remains a mystery that no one has an answer to. Nonetheless, it was designed and built that way for a reason. Someone on the inside obviously knew more about Presley's danger level than his fans, but sadly, the sleeping quarters were never built. If they had, Elvis would still be with us, and I wouldn't be writing this book.

As the investigators entered the room and turned to the right they discovered a large black bag on the bathroom counter. It was a leather doctor's bag. Nestled among the shaving cream, cologne and other personal articles they also noticed a book that had knocked over several items. For the moment they drew their attention to the black bag.

The front flap was open revealing its many compartments that would have been securely hidden if the bag were closed. As the men feasted their eyes on the bag, they were amazed to discover that all of its compartments were empty.

What could this mean? What could have been in the bag? Drugs? There was no evidence of drugs anywhere, not even a baby aspirin. Warlick began taking photographs. He took snapshots of the bag, the personal items on the counter, the book, the death scene and everything else of interest in the bathroom.

As he went into the other rooms to continue his photography, the other investigators examined the book. It was oddly strewn in the most conspicuous of locations, much like the two syringes they had found earlier.

Again, it was impossible to miss. As Warlick re-entered the bathroom with his photos, he joined his fellow investigators at the bathroom counter. Now, Warlick began examining the mysterious location of the book. At this time, Joe Esposito offered his version of where he found Presley's body.

Thompson and Cole's *The Death of Elvis* explains:

> *" He was found here,'* (said Esposito) *and pointed to the floor beyond the toilet. The body was found on its left side with its knees drawn up, and gold pajama bottoms down past his knees. Blood was in his nostrils, Esposito said. 'Are you sure about the position?' Warlick asked, mindful that this was a far cry from the version that Esposito had given at the hospital."*

As the investigators mentally struggled to decipher why Esposito had suddenly changed his entire story within less than two hours of Presley's death confirmation, their minds began to work on many other issues. *The Death of Elvis* continues:

> *"'(Al) Strada said Elvis was reading a book when he was stricken. It was laying open and face down on the counter among tumbled over cologne and after-shave bottles."*

Much to the contrary, Joe Esposito was telling a far different story – why? How could these two eyewitnesses be telling far different stories so quickly? Esposito told Warlick and the investigation team:

> *"Elvis was clutching the book in his hand when Esposito first saw him on the bathroom floor. Warlick considered how quick Esposito was to shade his facts and rejected his assertion."*

At this point in the investigation, Dan Warlick's veteran skills began putting the mental pieces of the puzzle together. Silently, he calculated that Esposito and Strada were telling very different stories. Even before any of the photos, facts or autopsy results had been analyzed, Esposito was telling multiple versions of what he allegedly saw and nothing added up. Esposito's odd nervousness also bothered the investigative team as their minds raced.

The changing stories regarding where Elvis was found, where the book that Elvis was reading ended up and the timeline itself, were in stark contrast to what Esposito had told everyone earlier that day, including a reporter in a TV interview at the hospital.

Why was he changing his mind about everything? Did he know more than he was saying? What would be the reason for him to withhold or scramble his information? Warlick soon asked the eye witnesses to the discovery, Joe Esposito, and Al Strada, if Elvis had aspirated or vomited in any way.

He was looking for any specimens or remaining evidence that could be further analyzed in the lab. This is all part of the rigorous stages of training investigators at this level go through, and Warlick was determined to be as thorough as possible.

The Death of Elvis covers this incident in great detail as Joe Esposito informed the investigators that the maids had also cleaned up the death scene, as well as the other rooms. Dan Warlick was furious! How could he be expected to do a thorough and complete investigation when all the evidence was gone? In *The Death of Elvis* Warlick surmised:

> *"Maybe the room had been cleaned with the best of intentions, the investigator rationalized. He didn't think so, but he didn't pursue the subject further."*

Struggling to get any insight or evidence, Warlick knelt down to the spot where Esposito had claimed Presley's head was upon discovery. There he noticed a moist spot in the carpeting. A quick sniff of the spot revealed the unmistakable whiff of vomit covered by the scent of detergent left by someone desperately attempting to mask the odor.

Then Warlick estimated the distance away from the toilet and surmised that he had not been given correct information, Elvis didn't fall off the toilet. In fact, the wet spot was over seven feet from the toilet. It became obvious that either he was not on the toilet at all, or had staggered a distance upon being stricken.

After the men had finished their investigation of the upstairs of Graceland, Dan Warlick interviewed Ginger Alden. She had obviously been crying but managed to proceed with the necessary details. She claimed that around 8:00 in the morning, Elvis was having trouble sleeping and went to the bathroom lounge area to read.

She told investigators that Elvis was reading a book on psychic energy. Within months her story changed and she identified the book as *Sex and Psychic Energy*. She later claimed that 'they' had told her not to identify the book, but she was careful not to say who *they* were.

Was it the same *they* that Vernon Presley mentioned as the investigators entered the house? ("They've taken him?") Or was it the same *they* that had Joe Esposito changing his story? The investigators mentally calculated the events of Graceland, gathered their findings and drove back to Baptist Memorial Hospital to speak with Shelby County Medical Examiner Jerry T. Francisco. They had many facts, but no answers.

Francisco was uninterested in their findings and turned his attention to readying the body for autopsy. Francisco was a veteran in his trade and had done this work thousands of times. By time Elvis Presley adorned Francisco's autopsy table, the good doctor had a minimum of 22 years of experience, including two separate medical residencies at hospitals in the local Memphis area.

By his credentials, he was by far the most qualified man to officiate the autopsy of Elvis Presley in the state of Tennessee. Meanwhile, the worldwide media, which was quite sparse by today's standards, coordinated television and radio transmissions in every country. Millions of radios, televisions and telephones suddenly came to life all at once as people tried to deal with Presley's death and the utter disbelief that accompanied it.

With news this shocking, no one was going to wait for tomorrow's newspaper headlines to get the truth, and everyone was on the telephone trying to find someone "in the know". The call lines of every radio and television station imaginable lit up like a Christmas tree and even stations that had the most state-of-the-art technology reported overloaded circuits as their networks buckled.

As the news spread across the globe, radio stations immediately ditched their planned programs and began a medley of Elvis' hits that lasted, in some cases, for days. While some stations organized impromptu tributes, others simply played his music at the request of the shocked fans.

Living in today's technology-laden world, it would be hard to imagine a time when, in 1977, news of the death of Elvis Presley had spread across the globe without Internet, cell phones, fax machines, 24-hour news networks and only three national television stations but travel it did.

This media phenomenon was almost as impossible to fathom as Presley's meteoric rise to fame itself. Nevertheless, with one-eighth of the media outlets that exist today, the news spread – news that everyone needed to know but no one wanted to hear.

Within minutes of the grim announcement, hundreds of fans had gathered outside the hospital, and at even more flocked to the gates of Presley's home. Meanwhile, back at Graceland, the phone rang continuously. Fellow celebrities, long-lost friends and even the heads of fan clubs around the world called to verify what they'd heard and offer condolences. Although many people were at Graceland, it was Elvis' father, Vernon Presley, that every caller wanted to speak with and they all asked the same question. What happened? The shocking death soon revealed an undeniable truth. The same Memphis Mafia that sheltered Elvis from the outside world also did a great job of sheltering the outside world from Elvis.

The general public had no idea how sick Elvis really was or that he was on a strict drug regimen. Tom Parker worked so hard over the years protecting Elvis' reputation that the general public was clueless. They never saw this coming.

The fans that had assembled themselves at Graceland's famous gate and its walled perimeter had drastically increased in numbers. They were suffering from a myriad of emotions. They were angry, heartbroken, sad, grief-stricken, ill and rife with disbelief.

Some were even suffering from sunstroke and needed emergency care. Regardless of their condition, everyone wanted answers and the Memphis police, who were attempting to control the crowd of thousands, secretly feared that if the cause of death wasn't acceptable, a riot would ensue.

Meanwhile, back at Baptist Memorial Hospital, investigator Warlick again tried to share his information from the death scene with Jerry Francisco. Again, he found the Medial Examiner uninterested, all but cutting him off in mid-sentence. Then, he asked Warlick if he would like to attend the autopsy. He didn't have to ask twice. Warlick immediately jumped at the chance.

Warlick slipped into a white laboratory coat and joined the autopsy team as they readied their gleaming instruments around Elvis's body. The scene was incredible. No less than nine doctors with a combination of 147 years of practical experience lined both sides of the porcelain autopsy table. Each doctor had his own area of expertise and was hand-picked to perform his specific duty in the dissection Elvis Presley's vital organs.

Among them were Dr. Eric Muirhead, Chief of Pathology at Baptist Memorial Hospital and a full Professor of Pathology at the University of Tennessee Medical School. Muirhead, in fact, was recognized as Francisco's senior, and was called in for his overall expertise in the field.

Even in death, Elvis Presley was treated like royalty, as they assembled the best and the brightest autopsy team that Tennessee had to offer. Once the procedure began, the enormity of what they were doing hit home. The lifeless chunk on the table wasn't Joe Shmoe, it was Elvis Presley. Less than 12 hours earlier, these men would have been asking for autographs, now they were preparing to cut Elvis' body apart. It was almost impossible to fathom.

The Rock-n-Roll rebel of the 1950s, and the idol of millions of fans around the world, was the lifeless, bulbous, blue/black corpse that was staring them blankly in the eyes. As the high-pitched clang of metal instruments rang in their ears, they were struck with the harsh reality that this was really about to happen. Elvis Presley was about to be cut to pieces. As the shock of the famous corpse slowly departed, Warlick got down to the usual business of inspecting the corpse.

Thompson and Cole's *The Death of Elvis* tells it like this:

> "Warlick checked Elvis' nose, observed a trickle of blood seeping from the nostrils...He did note that the body had 'congestion to the face and upper torso.' Warlick looked into Elvis' mouth. He saw the teeth had been smashed in the attempts to put a tube down Elvis' throat, but he saw no evidence of choking or vomiting. Putting these indicators together, the doctors estimated that Elvis might have died as early as 9:00 a.m."

Nearly two hours into the procedure, all of Elvis' organs had been removed, including his brain, which had meticulously sectioned and analyzed by pathologist Noel Florendo. Dr. Florendo was added to the team for his expertise with the electron microscope. Florendo remained at his work station analyzing the various tissue specimens that were presented to him by the other doctors.

The only time Florendo left his station was when it came time for Elvis' heart to be sectioned and analyzed. For this task, Dr. Florendo couldn't resist joining Warlick. The two men painstakingly cut every artery and chamber in Presley's heart at ¼ inch intervals. Piece by piece they inspected each portion but they still had no answers.

As the clock continued to tick and the sun fell on the extensive and ongoing post mortem probe, it became obvious that no answers would be established by the team until a later date. Incredibly, earlier in the day, Francisco had committed to a scheduled press conference at 8:00pm to reveal the cause of death.

As the world held its collective breath, the televised press conference began right on time. Francisco seated himself behind a long desk and adjusted his glasses.

He was still wearing his white lab coat which proved to be a nice effect for the public. As the cameras rolled, Francisco told the waiting world that Elvis Presley had died of *'cardiac arrhythmia due to undetermined heartbeat.'* In other words, Elvis died because his heart stopped beating.

Upon this comment, Dr. Muirhead, nearly fell over backwards. He simply couldn't believe what came out of Francisco's mouth. Why would he say such a thing before any samples could be tested or results tallied? Rather than tell the world that the autopsy was *"inconclusive pending further tests"*, Francisco told a bigger tale than Mother Goose.

The Death of Elvis covers Eric Muirhead's thoughts on Francisco's public announcement.

"Muirhead was aghast.", "What a silly diagnosis, he thought. The heart must stop beating before a person dies. And for the heart to stop, it goes into some kind of arrhythmia or irregular heartbeat.", "Surprisingly enough, the reason for the cardiac arrhythmia remained unknown and was reported to be brought on by "undetermined causes."

In the world of post-mortem investigation, this was lunacy. It took Theodore Curphey, Chief Coroner in the death of Marilyn Monroe, a full twelve days in 1962 to make such an announcement, but here was Francisco calling for a press conference a mere six hours after the discovery of the corpse?

Sidestep that for a moment and consider the crazy cause of death. These were hardly the actions of such a seasoned professional. Obviously there were other forces at work.

The next day, August 17th, Vernon Presley had the unbelievably difficult task of planning the funeral of his only child. He contacted Robert Kendall of the Memphis Funeral Home who arranged the funeral services for Elvis' mother nearly two decades prior. Vernon requested that his son be buried in a copper lined casket identical to the one he had selected for his wife. With Elvis being so close to his mother, he thought that would be a nice touch.

Beyond sentimental reasons, there were other motivations for this casket selection. Vernon knew that his son's death was very odd, and he was convinced that he had been murdered. This particular casket held special cylinders in it that would aid investigators in the event the Elvis' body needed to be exhumed.

Vernon was not the only one who thought in terms of solving the murder and finding the killer. Apparently, the funeral director also shared his belief. Back at Graceland, Elvis' devout fans sent enough flowers to sink the Titanic, which were lovingly placed on the front bank of the house for everyone to see.

The website www.Elvis.com claims;

> "Every blossom in Memphis had been sold by the afternoon of August 17, and additional flowers were shipped in from other parts of the country. It was the biggest day in the history of FTD, a florists' delivery service. FTD employees claim that more than 2,150 arrangements were delivered. The arrangements were shaped like lightning bolts, guitars, hound dogs and stars, as well as more traditional wreaths and bouquets."

The body was brought back to Graceland for family and a very select group of friends to view privately. It was during this time that one of Presley's cousins was paid $20,000 to secretly snap a photo of Elvis in his casket. The picture found its way onto the cover of the National Enquirer, making it the most famous issue ever printed.

After the family had their time alone with Elvis, they prepared for the public viewing, but nothing could possibly prepare them for what was coming. Presley's fans had poured in from all parts of the world and swelled the city's population to enormous levels. Hundreds of thousands of fans, and even members of the press, lined the streets of Memphis hoping to see the open casket which lay in state.

It quickly became obvious that it was impossible for everyone to see Elvis. The family even extended the hours to try to accommodate everyone but they still fell short of their goal. When the gates finally closed, 95,000 fans had passed by Elvis.

Some cried publicly, some cried privately, and some even brought their children along to join in the memorial spectacle. Elvis was well loved, and numerous celebrities attended his funeral. Some of the most notable celebrities on hand were Caroline Kennedy, Chet Atkins, Ann-Margaret, George Hamilton and Jackie Kahane. Regardless of their fame, there wasn't a dry eye in the house.

As the mourners, family members and celebrities made their way out of Graceland to the procession, it was time for the funeral director to get down to business. As the pallbearers stood in horror with tears rolling down their faces, the funeral workers started their process with great efficiency.

Without missing a step they removed the flowers and other sentimental objects. They cranked Elvis slowly downward to the bottom of the casket and folded the cloth linings in and around his face. Just before the lid closed for the last time, Elvis' friend, hairdresser, and spiritual advisor, Larry Geller, placed his hand on Presley's forehead for a moment.

He wanted to be the last person ever to touch Elvis – he was. As Geller pulled his hand back the lid closed and there wouldn't be another soul that would ever see Elvis Presley's face again.

Next, one of the funeral workers twisted the crank locking the lid closed and began to remove the decorative skirting that had been hiding the wheeled cart. While this was taking place, another worker removed the rows of huge flowers that had been assembled in a semi-circle around the box and began taking them to the procession.

With the path now cleared, all three workers rolled the casket to the door and the pallbearers took their designated places. By the hands of his closest friends Elvis was leaving his living room for the very last time. Within minutes, the gates of Graceland slowly opened and a sparkling white Cadillac hearse quietly slipped though, followed in sequence by sixteen white Cadillac limousines.

The fans that lined both sides of the highway stood in sunburned grief as the saga they never thought they'd see unfolded before their eyes. As the hearse coasted down the street, all flags were flown at half-mast on the order of Tennessee governor Ray Blanton. It was Elvis Presley's last ride.

Vernon was grief-stricken and crying, but he was also furious. He quietly burned in his seat. He understood that among the mourners were people who knew more than they were saying. He also knew that this was well planned, and that the bad actors had help - help from the inside.

3
The Questions

"'total, complete, unmitigated bullshit."

-Dan Warlick, The Death of Elvis-

Immediately, there were questions being asked about the validity of what Dr. Francisco had told the media. Francisco, the physician who signed the death certificate, publicly stated that Elvis died of "cardiac arrhythmia," or an erratic heartbeat.

The flash prognosis was nothing more than a juicy medical term for the media to chew on so they would go away - and it worked like a charm.

To begin with, it is medically impossible for anyone in the post-mortem universe to diagnose that a human heart was beating irregularly. For that diagnosis to happen the heart would have needed to be beating in the first place.

Since Francisco never examined Presley's heart when it was beating, it would have been impossible for him to have given such a diagnosis.

The second problem with Francisco's prognosis of "cardiac arrhythmia" was that everyone's heart beats erratically when they die. Have you ever seen a corpse with a heart that continued to beat normally?

Me either. Since it would have been impossible for Francisco to determine "cardiac arrhythmia" on a dead person, listing it as the cause of death because the heart stopped should be listed as everyone's cause of death.

Francisco may as well have said that Elvis Presley died from rigor mortis. Both cardiac arrhythmia and rigor mortis happen to everyone when they die.

Furthermore, how could (or would) he make such an outrageous announcement, even if it were possible, without a completed autopsy, tests of Elvis' tissue samples, or taking into account Warlick's evidence from the death scene?

The very idea that Jerry Francisco, a seasoned and highly educated medical examiner, would do such a thing is an incredible sacrilege to the medical profession.

With all of that being said, it was obvious that his mind was made up before Elvis was even on the autopsy table. But why? Why would Francisco do such a thing? After all, people just don't lie for the sake of lying, and they don't cover up the facts unless there is something worth covering up.

Was Jerry Francisco on the take? Was he paid by someone to lie about the results? Was he threatened by someone? Was this the reason behind his odd behavior? Ponder those questions as the book continues.

While I can't make any assertions about Francisco, what I can state with absolute confidence and certainty is that people tend to believe the first official version of a story. That is a researched fact. Politicians know this well and practice it to the point where our news is nothing more than repeated political spin.

This easy to accomplish when America had the funeral of investigative journalism in the late 1980's. There is no greater example of this than the people who believe that Bill Clinton smoked marijuana in college but didn't inhale. After this statement, the American people had no trouble electing the pot-smoking President to two terms.

It is also a fact that if lies are repeated with enough frequency eventually everyone will begin to accept them as the gospel truth. It's surprising to realize that very few people in today's high-tech society actually "think" and form their own opinions.

For the most part we have become a society of canaries just repeating what we have been told or hear on television. Marketing, Advertising, and Public Relations professionals know this very well, and apparently so did Dr. Francisco.

Francisco was a very smart man and was attempting to create his own spin on the cause of Elvis Presley's death. For whatever reason or motivation it was his intention to create a story that he thought would be spread by the media and repeated throughout the world for generations. He failed.

In fact, he failed with such a thud that in 1979, a mere two years after he unsuccessfully tried to associate cardiac arrhythmia to Presley's cardiovascular disease, ABC News was hot on the trail. The ABC News television show 20/20, with its host, Geraldo Rivera, began to dig mightily into the death of Elvis Presley with the assistance of two Memphis based investigators, James Cole and Charles Thompson.

The research that Thompson, Cole and Rivera performed remains the holy grail of facts on the subject, and as they began to dig, Francisco's jigsaw puzzle began to quickly lose its pieces.

In Thompson and Cole's book, *The Death of Elvis*, Rivera began tracking down and independently interviewing those involved in the autopsy. The first person he attempted to get information from was Jerry Francisco himself. He was unsuccessful, reporting the following on his television show:

> *"The key to the mystery is the Shelby County Medical Examiner Dr. Jerry T. Francisco and if we had his help we could have cracked this case months ago but we did not. He consistently refused to be interviewed by us claiming that the information was confidential. He also refused to make public the autopsy results that would lay to rest once and forever the controversy over how and why Elvis Presley died. In order to obtain the results, we filed a lawsuit against Dr. Jerry T. Francisco. Our motives are simple, based on the evidence you are about to see we believe there has been a cover-up."*

Rivera and ABC News had uncovered enough information through their lawsuit to probe deeper into the case and that meant conducting further interviews with some very key people. Next on their list was Dr. Noel Florendo.

If we remember, Dr. Florendo was the pathologist who personally inspected the sectioned pieces of Presley's heart. The organ was carefully dissected by Dan Warlick and Dr. Thomas Chesney in the presence of all nine doctors in the autopsy room. Dr. Florendo, an expert with the electron microscope had an impeccable reputation among his peers. He was beyond the best person to perform that task.

With Francisco's credibility now in question, arranging a meeting with Florendo was the next logical step in their probe. Rivera and his 20/20 team located him a few days later. He had taken up residency at another area hospital and he agreed to be interviewed on camera. During the interview, Florendo admitted that he was indeed shocked at Francisco's announcement and was not at all in agreement with it.

The interview went as follows:

Rivera: *"Dr. Florendo, in your medical judgment, was there any evidence that Elvis Presley died of a heart attack?"*

Florendo: *"There was no gross evidence of a heart attack. "*

Rivera: "Were you surprised by Dr. Jerry Francisco's announcement on the night of the autopsy that Elvis died of cardiac arrhythmia?"

Florendo: "Personally, yes. I was surprised."

Rivera: "What is cardiac arrhythmia?"

Florendo: "Cardiac arrhythmia is best described as an irregular heartbeat, sufficiently irregular enough to cause death."

Rivera: "And in Elvis Presley's case"?

Florendo: "I could not find enough evidence to substantiate cardiac arrhythmia."

Rivera: "So Elvis didn't die of a heart attack?"

Florendo: "In my opinion, I did not see any evidence of a heart attack morphemically."

Rivera: "Morphemically, meaning?"

Florendo: "Meaning there was no gross evidence of a heart attack."

    In my meeting with Dan Warlick in November of 2017, immediately before I started to rewrite this book and update its contents for the five year anniversary of its original release date in 2013, and a full forty years after death and resulting autopsy, Warlick, who hadn't seen Florendo in years, still held him in the highest possible regard.

Warlick said of Florendo: *"I don't know where he is today, I haven't seen him in years but he was a straight arrow and a very good doctor."* Judging by Florendo's interview with Rivera and ABC's 20/20 news crew, I would have to agree with him.

Florendo saw no evidence of a heart attack and he wasn't alone. Investigator Warlick was no stranger to post mortem procedures. He knew what clogged arteries looked like, and he saw none of them that day.

While it was true that the Presley's heart was enlarged, it had no clogged arteries, and at only 42 years of age, he was years away from heart disease or other such complications.

Medical facts don't lie, and upon receiving the information that had been supplied by these two doctors, reality hit me. Everyone around the world had been lied to, and so the mystery continues. Why did Francisco lie? Who held enough power over him to make him lie? If that wasn't puzzling and disturbing enough, there is a bigger question that must be answered.

Since Presley's heart hadn't failed him due to cardiac arrhythmia as the press-conference suggested, and there was no evidence of clogged arteries or heart disease, what exactly killed Elvis? Since there are only a limited number of things that can happen to a heart that can cause a natural death, we can now rule out a heart attack.

As we move forward with the probe, keep in mind that whatever killed Elvis happened quickly, as he only had a few minutes to struggle. He died only a few feet from the point where he had been stricken.

Amazingly, nothing was found in any of Presley's organs that would have caused the immediate death that he experienced. In discussing this with Warlick, he relayed to me that Elvis' brain and other organs in question had been carefully sectioned and analyzed and there was no sign of stroke, or an embolism. There are only four "Modes of Death", or, in layman's terms, ways a person can die.

They are: Natural Causes, Suicide, Accidental Death, and Murder. Since his death wasn't brought on by an issue with his heart, brain, or any random embolism, and whatever killed Elvis hit him quickly, at this point in the investigation we have successfully ruled out mode of death number one, death by natural causes.

With natural causes now officially debunked, we must continue to investigate the other three modes: accidental death, suicide and murder. Thompson, Cole and Rivera probed accidental death during their exhaustive investigation at great length. After interviewing several members of the Baptist Memorial Hospital staff privately and off-camera, Rivera issued the following statement to his 20/20 viewing public:

> *"A highly placed source within Baptist Memorial Hospital confirmed that Elvis Presley died from a condition known as polypharmacy. He died from an accidental overdose of prescription medicine*

– *legal medicine prescribed by licensed doctors."*

Could this be true? Could this solve the mystery of what killed Elvis Presley? Dr. Herald Sexton, one of the doctors at the autopsy, had been charged with the responsibility of gathering specimens of Presley's organs for testing. At that time, Baptist Memorial Hospital, although a very large and state-of-the-art facility, had no toxicology lab to properly test these samples.

Dr. Francisco had given orders that samples be sent to a local university for toxicology testing, and they were. However, unbeknownst to Francisco, Dr. Sexton had sent his own samples for testing. The secret samples that were sent were done for two reasons. The first reason was to explore a curious comment that Elvis' valet, Al Strada, had muttered to the EMTs: *"We think he OD'd."*

The second reason, and perhaps the more pressing issue, was that the outside world was now beginning to doubt the professionalism of the doctors who performed the autopsy, thanks to Dr. Francisco and his ridiculous cause of death.

One of the laboratories that Dr. Sexton had sent his samples to was a neighboring facility on the other side of the city, which tested urine only – standard in this type of an investigation.

The facility performed a full drug screening on the specimens, much like what is done today for pre-employment testing. The results came back in conflict with Dr. Francisco's laboratory test results, which tested both blood and urine.

Thompson and Cole, in *The Death of Elvis*, explain the results:

> "[Dr. Sexton's] Tests were positive for four types of depressants - barbiturates, meprobamate, benzodiazepines and ethchlorvynol. They were negative for a host of other types, including amphetamine, cocaine and notably morphine and codeine."

> "In contrast, Francisco's toxicology lab at the University of Tennessee issued a report a few days later randomly combining test results from both blood and urine. The UT work-up identified ethinamate, methaqualone, codeine, meperidine, chlorpheniramine and unspecified barbiturates as being present in either blood or urine. It reported all of those drugs as being in concentrations "less than toxic or lethal levels,"

After several days of infighting and turmoil between the hospital elite, Dr. Francisco, and the media, Dr. Sexton sought to settle the issue by secretly contacting the best laboratory in the country. This highly rated, state-of-the-art facility was located on the other side of the nation and specialized in testing not only urine and blood, but frozen tissue samples as well. It was named BioScience Laboratories.

After making the necessary phone calls, Dr. Sexton carefully packed Elvis Presley's tissue samples in dry ice, labeled them with a phony name and shipped them off to California. In constant telephone contact with the laboratory, Dr. Sexton explained that this was a high-profile case and the handling of this material needed to be of a critical nature.

Although the name on the samples was not Elvis Presley, the cat was pretty much out of the bag. After all, here was a doctor from the same hospital that was now known as Presley's *"death hospital,"* suddenly contacting their laboratory with a high-profile case?

The coincidence was too much for the people on the receiving end of the frozen specimens to bear, but they played along with the game at hand. The key element of the autopsy report, which Harold Sexton wanted in the open, is the summary of Bioscience's findings which indicated that *"Codeine was present at levels approximately ten times those concentrations found therapeutically."*

The overall conclusion as to what killed Elvis Presley, according to Thompson, Cole, and Geraldo Rivera, came to them first from Presley's nurse, Marian Cocke, and later from Presley's former girlfriend Linda Thompson. Both had told investigators that Presley was allergic to Codeine. They claimed that he broke out in a rash and became short of breath which panicked him.

What they were describing was something named *Anaphylactic shock. Anaphylactic shock* is a widespread and very serious allergic reaction which is also known as *Anaphylaxis*. These reactions vary depending on the circumstances involved and the amount of antigen in the body.

The allergic reaction ranges from mild to serious and includes: dizziness, loss of consciousness, labored breathing, swelling of the tongue and breathing tubes, blueness of the skin, low blood pressure, heart failure, and even death.

On the heels of ABC's probe and 20/20's lead investigator, Geraldo Rivera, Thompson and Cole's final conclusion as to what killed Elvis in their book was that Elvis mistakenly took Codeine (little white pills) thinking that they were Dilaudid (little yellow pills).

Thompson and Cole surmised that Elvis took Codeine by accident, and began to have an allergic reaction while he was on the toilet. His shortness of breath panicked him and he began to struggle, throwing his book aside. They claim that Elvis died from an accidental overdose of drugs.

This is a plausible scenario, since their book also explains that Elvis didn't die quickly, and there were four obvious conditions that indicated vessel hemorrhaging, which indicated that Elvis struggled to live:

"...forensic experts outside of Francisco's office noted ample evidence for concluding that when stricken, Elvis didn't die instantly. The suppressed autopsy report stresses four points: (1) Minor edema, or accumulation of fluid, was found in the lungs; (2) there was petechie, or small hemorrhages, from the line of demarcation at the abdomen up to the neck; (3) there were signs of conjunctivitis or an edema-type condition around the eyes; and (4) there was cyanotic or bluish condition around the abdomen from lack of oxygen in the blood. All four indicated that Elvis had lived for a short time, allowing the vessels to hemorrhage."

This was a very good theory produced by the digging of three very capable men. All were veteran reporters, and the latter two were Memphis natives, which allowed them a backstage pass to certain areas others wouldn't have had.

The book they wrote was a masterpiece of information; however, there were people within the medical community both in and out of Memphis that disagreed and flatly doubted their labor-intensive findings.

One of the doubters was none other than investigator Dan Warlick himself. He believed that drugs played a role but were not the cause of death. Another doubter of Thompson and Cole's accidental overdose theory was the previously discredited Shelby County Medical Examiner Jerry Francisco.

Dr. Francisco claimed that people who succumb to a drug death are found in a position of comfort, and Presley was not. He was found in an awkward position on the floor. Meanwhile, in Las Vegas, Dr. Elias Ghanem, one of Presley's regular doctors when he was on tour, told his friends he was certain Elvis had fallen off the toilet and suffocated in the thick shag carpet.

Ghanem's reasoning for this assumption was the report Presley's protruding tongue that was nearly bitten in two. Forensic Pathologist Dr. Cyril Wecht when presented with material to review by Rivera said the following;

> "the level [of codeine] was significant by itself. It could have resulted in death. It was near the fatal level. On the other hand, if he had been taking it for some time, he would have built up some tolerance."

Dr. Wecht, as always, was speaking truthfully, and I was flattered during the writing of this book to have had correspondence with him. It is unfortunate that he wasn't at the autopsy, and the only thing he had to base his findings on were someone else's toxicology reports.

While in repeated communication with Dr. Wecht on this project, my overriding feeling was that he would have loved to be presented with something to test independently. It obviously made him feel uncomfortable taking someone else's test result as gospel.

There is nothing that I would love more than to present Cyril with tissue, urine or blood samples, but unfortunately, that is impossible. Such evidence has been long since discarded by those in charge of Baptist Memorial Hospital, and the body remains buried under a huge slab of granite and bronze in meditation gardens at Graceland.

Even if we exhumed Elvis Presley's body, after more than forty years, there would be almost nothing left to test. Not that testing the scant remains would be impossible, but at best, it would be extremely difficult to ensure the quality of the results.

Quite possibly the only thing that could be achieved by exhuming Elvis, would be to test the DNA of the remains, which would finally put to rest the ongoing lore that he faked his death and that a wax figure was in the casket. Beyond that, it's a pond that is not worth fishing in.

Fictitious wax dummy aside, two distinct things are known of Elvis Presley that are absolutely factual. During the autopsy it was discovered and well documented that all of his organs were very large, bordering on enormous.

The second thing was that he had an incredible tolerance for the prescription drugs that he was taking, and these two facts connect. Larger internal organs can handle larger quantities. This is why women who drink the same amount of alcohol as a man will become intoxicated faster. Their internal organs are smaller by nature and they cannot process the alcohol as fast.

The same applies for high doses of prescription drugs. It is also well documented that when the human body is steadily enhanced via any form of internal or external activity, be it drugs or exercise, it eventually begins to build up a tolerance and requires a higher dose to be effective.

In fact, this is how muscles are built. Bodybuilders who have huge arms must maintain a strict regimen of specific exercises to continually tax the muscles, either by adding weight or through higher repetition. The body's response is to build up the muscle to match the intensity of the training, thus requiring a more intense workout.

In short, the muscle builds a tolerance and requires more to affect it. The resulting adaptation is a bigger muscle that needs yet a more intense workout. This is the same way that martial artists can smash their hands through wood boards, bricks and even concrete blocks in defiance of everything the medical community would deem possible.

This is accomplished by years of repetitious pounding which conditions the hand to do things beyond the normal limits of logic. I've even seen a man put four fingers through a piece of drywall.

The result was four little holes and an amazed crowd. Medical science would consider this to be an impossible and lethal move for your fingers, but some people in the martial arts world do it on a daily basis.

The man eventually revealed his secret. The method was exactly the same as muscle building or breaking bricks in Karate. He "tolerance trained" by jamming his fingers into buckets that were half filled with sand, hitting the bottom every time.

When sand became of no challenge after thousands and thousands of repetitions, he replaced the sand with beans, then wet sand, and finally hard clay. When he could hit the bottom of a bucket with hard clay every time, after many months and even years of training, he knew that he could put his fingers easily through drywall.

This is also the case with heavy drinkers. They drink so much, so often, that they continually need more and more to reach the same level of intoxication. This is why some alcoholics switch from beer to vodka, for example.

The chemicals are different, and since their body is not immune to the new chemical, they can get a buzz faster. The same is true in every sense for drug takers, like Elvis.

Different drugs do different things, and you can only take them for so long before your system builds up a tolerance that requires more and more pills be taken. According to Joe Esposito, and various others in Elvis' entourage, Elvis had been taking prescription drugs, in some capacity, beginning in the late 1960's until his death in 1977.

In reality, there was nothing normal about Elvis Presley's decade of drug use and increasing tolerance. Most likely, one-third of Elvis' nightly dose would have put any one of us in the morgue, but to Elvis, with his larger than normal internal organs and his decade of intense tolerance building, the dose was routine.

The additional medication necessary for Elvis to maintain his effect would be so high that one of his usual doses probably would have been classified as lethal to a regular person, and the ranges in toxicology were set up to measure the tolerances of normal people.

To solidify this point, enter once again, the comments of Dr. Cyril Wecht. As he continued to discuss the death in that now-famous 1979 interview with 20/20's Geraldo Rivera, Wecht validated this by stating the following:

> *"On the other hand, if he had been taking it for some time, he would have built up some tolerance."*

In an undated television interview by *The Insider* posed similar questions to both Elvis' doctor, Dr. Nichopoulos and Dan Warlick. In the interview, Dr. Nichopoulos stated the following when asked about Presley's alleged drug addiction.

The interview went as follows:

Interviewer: *"Did you over prescribe medication to Elvis Presley?*

Dr. Nick: *"Elvis wanted these prescriptions in his name so his daddy wouldn't raise hell with him for spending money for somebody else, so all of this was written in his name, it looked like he was taking all these medicines and he wasn't. I mean, Elvis never even had control of his medications.*

I kept all his medicines, I not only kept them but I hired a nurse to stay out there with him to handle his medicines, so he never had them, he never had control of his medicines."

Interviewer: *"Do you or did you ever regret giving Elvis all of the pills that he had been taking and that you've prescribed at any point, did you regret it?"*

Dr. Nick: *"No, I don't regret anything that I gave him. I think they were medical necessities. I think we were treating diseases."*

During this interview several things became obvious to me. Not only was Dr. Nick picking his words carefully, but he was also struggling not to say too much about Presley's medical conditions that he was treating.

Even the death of a patient doesn't give Dr. Nick, or any doctor, the right to violate the sacred doctor's oath of "doctor / patient confidentiality." It was obvious that what he was saying and what he wanted to say were two different things. He desperately wanted to tell the world what he was prescribing and what diseases and illness he was treating, but he simply couldn't.

In my personal meeting with Dan Warlick, he corroborated the assertions of the doctor. He told me that prescriptions were written for Presley's entire Memphis Mafia, under Elvis' name as Presley's father, Vernon, had taken control of Elvis' finances, and Elvis didn't want to get an earful.

Elvis was a very generous man who lavished his friends' with gold rings, watches, Cadillacs, and even houses. He probably did this, in part, due his kind nature as a human being, and possibly as a repayment for them being loyal to him and remaining his close friends through high school when he and his music were picked on.

For whatever reason, Presley's generosity remains unmatched to this day and his lavish spending was something that his father struggled to keep a lid on. Warlick stated that:

> *"The pills would be in a bowl in the room, like a sugar bowl, and all of the guys would take whatever they needed, and if there were two or three pills left they might give them to Elvis."*

Over the years Warlick had forged a close personal friendship with one of Elvis' employees, Al Strada, who found Elvis' corpse. Strada also corroborated what Warlick and Dr. Nick had asserted, claiming that the community bowl of pills had taken place on a regular basis.

Just because Elvis had been prescribed all of those pills certainly doesn't mean that he was the one taking them. Indeed he was not. His entire inner circle of friends had a drug problem that was supplied out of the community bowl of drugs written under Elvis' name. Writing such a prescription was questionable conduct by Dr. Nick but understandable given the circumstances.

This was a time before people realized the dangers of such medications, and years before such things as the Betty Ford clinic. Simply stated, it would have been physically impossible for any human being to ingest the amount of medication that was prescribed to Elvis Presley during that period of time, regardless of the size of the internal organs or their tolerance.

To continue with the interview with Dr. Nichopolous the interviewer asks, *"Was he drug addict?* Dr. Nick responded:"

> *"There was only one time for sure that I knew he was a drug addict, and that was a time when he flew into Memphis after he had a series of acupuncture treatments from a doctor in California."*

> *"The doctor had sold him on bill of goods that he was going to clear up his back pain and clear up that pain doing this acupuncture, but he wasn't using acupuncture needles."*

> *"He was using syringes, and the syringes had Demerol in them and Cortisone with xylocaine, which was a local anesthetic. Of course you he always felt better after that, I mean, he talked some of the other guys into going to the same acupuncturist because he was so good."*

Later in the interview, Dan Warlick was questioned as to why there was such a controversy surrounding Presley's death.

He responds:

> "The reason there was so much controversy was that you had a committee of pathologists with two different views. Medical Examiner's or forensic pathologists who want only to come up with an accurate, sustainable and provable cause of death and manner of death. A cause of death for example might be drowning but that may be an accidental drowning, a suicidal drowning, or unknown. So the two things a forensic pathologists would look at, generally speaking hospital pathologists, are listing all the organic problems and disease processes they identified."

> "There was no initial and acute cause of death, clearly established, so then it came down to lab testing. We had several labs testing the samples from the Presley autopsy, and they were somewhat consistent in their results, but none of their results established a baseline of medications or byproducts of medications in Elvis Presley that were even toxic."

> "Those medications are found in different levels: Absent, or trace, or therapeutic, and the next level is toxic, that level makes you sick, and the final level is lethal. In the Presley autopsy there were no lethal levels nor were there any toxic levels. So for the first time to my knowledge in medical history the diagnosis was formulated by

the pathologist from the hospital that it was a poly pharmacy. I think they may have even coined that term but I'm not sure, but they felt like a combination of those drugs in the absence of any other cause of death was a probable cause of death, but of course that autopsy has never been made public. "

"And Dr. Francisco, who was the state medical examiner, and the county medical examiner, determined it was a natural death because of a very large sick heart, with a history of heart problems, hospitalizations, and also because the investigation at the scene, which did not indicate that this was an overdose death at all, so two different views, and since it was cloaked in secrecy, there was no clear cut answer."

To further dispute Thompson and Cole's theory of an accidental or even intentional overdose, we need to look no further than their own book. On the bottom of page 61 is the description from Dan Warlick as he checks Elvis' body for allergic reactions - none were found.

"Dan Warlick examined Elvis's larynx, the voice box, situated between the base of the tongue and the windpipe or trachea. The larynx contains two bands of tissue called the vocal cords, which make speech and singing possible. The sounds are created by the expansion and contraction of the vocal cords as air passes through them. Warlick was checking for edema. He was looking for swelling in the larynx – an indicator

that Elvis had suffered an allergic reaction to drugs."

Aside from the obvious contradictions between the findings of Presley's corpse, and the theory of a drug death, there were other reasons why an overdose simply was not possible.

Numerous friends, members of the Memphis Mafia, as well as Elvis' personal Doctor, Dr. Nichopolous, have been well documented as saying that Elvis knew more about pills than a pharmacist. This was well covered in at least two books referenced below by men that were at Presley's side on a regular and daily basis. Jerry Schilling in *Elvis: Murdered by the Mob* noted:

> *"He would look them up in the Physicians' Desk Reference and try to discover what he should take." And Sonny West in Elvis: What Happened? notes: "He has got medical dictionaries on the pills and he knows the color codes. Show him a pill or tell him its color on the capsule, and he can identify it in a second. I have seen him with literally dozens of bottles of every different kind of pill. Now, he knows what pill to mix with another pill. He knows the dosages and the exact result."*

It would be impossible for Elvis Presley, a studied and veteran pill-popper, to become confused between two little yellow pills (Dilaudid) and two little white pills (Codeine) and as suggested. But, to run the full theory out for nothing more than argument's sake, let's further expand and analyze the possibility of polypharmacy. First, take for granted that some other source didn't add the mega dose of Codeine to the toxicology report from BioScience Laboratories, to easily fabricate a cause of death when they figured out who the patient was, or strong arm the laboratory itself into doing so.

But remember, there were no signs of an allergic reaction upon Warlick's inspection of the corpse – absolutely none, and Elvis Presley was very allergic to Codeine. This explains why Warlick wasn't in agreement with Thompson or Cole's cause of Elvis' death. Codeine could not have caused the singers death as there was none in his corpse. So how did it magically appear in the toxicology report? Where the hell did it come from?

In 1979, ABC News and their show 20/20 had been experiencing lackluster ratings and they were weeks away from being canceled. Each and every time they revisited the subject of Elvis Presley's death they enjoyed a huge ratings spike. Did Geraldo Rivera's investigative team fabricate the toxicology report by BioScience Laboratories and give it to Dr. Cyril Wecht to get better ratings?

Did the network glom off Dr. Wecht's credibility to increase the sensationalism of the subject matter? Anyone who has lived through the media and political landscape of the Clinton–Trump Presidential election is well aware of what fake news is. Was the cocktail of drugs in the toxicology report, including the vanishing codeine dose, just another fake news story?

Putting all of that aside, since the position of Elvis' body had not been in a "position of comfort," which would indicate to authorities a drug death by polypharmacy, he hadn't had an allergic reaction to any medication as indicated by the examination of the corpse itself, and the death scene investigation hadn't yielded any drugs, an accidental drug death can be ruled out as second mode of death. Elvis Presley did not die of an accidental overdose of drugs.

With both natural and an accidental removed as possible causes of death, we have to address the third mode of death: suicide. An excerpt taken from a television special by *A Current Affair* which aired on November 19th 1990 stated the following regarding the possibility that Elvis had killed himself. The brief transcript of their video begins with the narrator:

> *"In recent months author Albert Goldman and Elvis' step-brother David Stanley claimed to have evidence that Elvis committed suicide. An extract from an updated biography was published in* LIFE Magazine. *One motive driving the suicide theory: Elvis had felt betrayed in the months prior to his death by former aides, among them Red West who had been a bodyguard. Dr. Nichopoulos discounts the suicide theory..."*

When interviewed by *A Current Affair* about the possibility that Elvis had committed suicide, Dr. Nichopoulos said the following:

> *"I think it's a big zero. For one, I don't think Elvis was capable of committing suicide. Two, he had too many other opportunities to commit suicide*

at much more stressful times than what were going on at the time of his death, when he really had access to drugs, more than what he had when he died. I think Elvis, at this time, was reorganizing his life."

The last sentence of Dr. Nick's quote speaks volumes about the frame of mind Elvis was in as July turned to August of 1977. While it was true that Tom Parker and Elvis Presley had an agreement of a 50/50 partnership split, and they would divide all of the profits equally, the evolution Presley's music, his growing friend base, and his generosity were taking a financial toll on the king.

Out of Elvis' 50%, he had to pay all of the Memphis Mafia, all of his band members, an entire orchestra, a vocalist quartet, all of the planes and numerous 18-wheelers necessary for his traveling roadshow. If that wasn't enough, according to the original agreement, he still had to pay for all of Tom Parker's business expenses.

This was no easy feat for a man who had signed away all of his music royalty rights four years prior, or a man who was the biggest tax payer in the state of Tennessee. Literally the only income Elvis Presley had in 1977 came from the labor intensive and very hectic tours that had him frantically racing from city to city, covering hundreds of miles in between.

In other words, despite his best efforts Elvis was performing himself into poverty. To try and ease the financial bleeding, Elvis' father had taken over his finances and had started to make cutbacks.

At first the cutbacks were minor. The guys were asked to stop drinking a certain type of bottled water because it was imported and it was very expensive. Then, the cutbacks started to get bigger, eventually leading to the firing of three bodyguards: Sonny West, Red West and Dave Hebler.

These three men were three of the toughest bodyguards Elvis had, and their firing by Vernon wasn't popular among the three men. Unfortunately, these were the same three men who were also creating a ton of liability issues for Elvis, as they were too rough with his fans. People who just wanted an autograph were getting unnecessarily roughed up and bloodied just for getting close to him.

This not only made Elvis look bad, but a few of the victims had filed suit against the Presley family. Firing these three men was Vernon's way of killing two birds with one stone, which on the surface looked like a great idea, but just below the surface bad blood was brewing.

Vernon's financial planning also included persuading Elvis to change his last will and testament excluding everyone close to him, with the exception of his father and his daughter. The catalyst behind the decision was Vernon's divorce from his second wife. Vernon wanted Dee Stanley's boys: Ricky, David and Billy, some of Elvis' old friends since childhood, and even a few of his closest cousins written out of the will. Immediately after this happened, word spread like wildfire among his inner circle as disgruntled friends and relatives soon came out of the woodwork resulting in some ugly confrontations.

While most of the anger eventually dissipated when they heard the reasoning behind the change, there were a few selfish people who sought revenge. From the aforementioned television interview, Dr. Nick explains:

> "At the time of his death there were two wills, the will that was probated and the will that wasn't probated, which was his real will." - "There are people that seriously think that there were motives in the change of the will that would have made one capable of doing away with Elvis."

This bad blood among the people in Elvis' inner circle, the same people who had access to him on a daily basis, leaves us no alternative. We must explore the fourth and final mode of death – Murder.

Having stated that, there exists no way to discredit Thompson and Cole's book, *The Death of Elvis*. It is a masterpiece that took an enormous amount of time to research, gather, organize and write, but, by their own admission in the book, they doubted they would ever find the true cause of death:

> "Even with the autopsy results finally in hand, Thompson and Cole still weren't satisfied that they knew what really happened to cause Elvis' death."

Their dead end really wasn't their fault. The information they needed to crack this case wasn't available to the public when their book was published in 1991. Also, there would have been no way for them to gather the information they needed from Jerry T. Francisco and the other doctors involved, who were under strict orders to gag and twist as much information as humanly possible.

To add to the mystery, everyone in Graceland was telling different stories, at different times, and changing their facts. So, here we have multiple people, with ample access to Elvis, all with an axe to grind and all of them twisting their facts. Ok, stop. Put the book down. Take a pause and think about this for a minute.

The same people who had just been written of Elvis Presley's will were not telling the truth about the facts and circumstances surrounding his death? Didn't you just have that Wile E. Coyote moment? Didn't an anvil just fall on your head?

If you combine all this, with a death scene that was mysteriously sanitized before an investigation could take place, with at least three conflicting stories as to the position and location of the discovery of Elvis' body, you can quickly deduce that each and every one of these people are lying.

The November 19th 1990 interview on *A Current Affair* with Dr. Nichopoulos continues:

> "*As far as Elvis' death is concerned, I had never entertained the idea that Elvis had committed suicide, but murder was entertained… Shortly after Elvis' death* (name intentionally bleeped by editor) *went around and told several people and had stated that he had killed Elvis.* "

"My initial speculation was that this was not true. That the information I had to put into my computer was that (name intentionally bleeped by editor) *was high on drugs and could have been hallucinating or whatever. I discussed with Elvis' father, Vernon, the possibility of something else happening other than an overdose or a heart attack or whatever and Vernon had this burning desire that Elvis was killed."*

Vernon didn't just suspect that Elvis had been murdered. He knew Elvis was murdered because he knew more about what was going on behind the scenes. No casual observer knew of the mob entanglements, lawsuits and genuine bad blood between those in high positions, or how those inside Presley's Memphis Mafia aided his death and set the stage for one of the most secretive murders in American history.

Since the publication of Thompson and Cole's book, new evidence surfaced that shows in great certainty that despite their tireless efforts, they hadn't even uncovered half the story. Elvis wasn't having drug problems – he was having thug problems.

Elvis began to experience security problems and death threats in the late 1960s. It was around this time that the iron-caged window boxes began to be installed at Graceland, and on Colonel Parker's house as well. While Parker began to invest his money in elaborate alarm systems, Elvis turned Graceland into a fortress and gathered an obscene number of weapons.

The need for the added security was well documented in numerous books including *Elvis: What Happened?* and *Elvis: Murdered by the Mob*. Both clearly state that in the late 1960's Elvis' life was in great danger as extortion plots and death threats became more and more numerous.

The most serious of these threats came in a two-pronged package. While performing in Las Vegas one of Presley's friends received a threat that someone was going to kidnap and assassinate Elvis. This madness continued until Presley's new security policy slowly began to turn Graceland into a fortress. A compound, much like the one you would find in the *Godfather* movies, complete with stone walls, 24-hour armed guards, bars on the windows, security monitors, and countless assault weapons and handguns at the ready.

Unbeknownst to Elvis, the times when his safety was threatened coincided with the times when Colonel Parker's gambling debts were either too high, or completely unpaid. Life slowly started to change for Elvis. Soon, there would be no more casual walks down to the fence on weekends to let the fans into Graceland.

Gone were the days where he would ride his horse down to the gate to sign autographs on a whim, and the days of little Lisa Marie's golf cart dalliances started to become a thing of the past as well. This carefree life had been replaced by fear, armed guards, and weapons.

An expert from the book *Elvis: What Happened?* elaborates: "It is February, 1976, and Red West is summoned to Presley's bedroom in Graceland. He knocks, enters and is taken aback at a huge arsenal of guns lying on the floor. 'The floor was just covered with automatic weapons, pistols, rifles, rockets. There was every kind of weapon there except tanks and bazookas. I've never seen so much hardware in my life.'"

In the end, all of Presley's guns, armed guards, and security cameras would be useless to him as his murderers came at him with smiles. How else do you explain the death of a man who was just given *"an extensive physical five days before (death) and found in fit condition"*? This was the comment made by Dr. Nichopoulos and found in the research of Thompson and Cole's *The Death of Elvis*.

A similar comment was published regarding Presley's clean bill of health in the book *Elvis: What Happened?* In the book, there is a printed transcript of a telephone conversation between Red West and Elvis. The following comment was made by Elvis himself:

> "I just had an absolute physical, head to toe, in the last three weeks. One of those things that is required by Lloyds of London."

So, how is it possible for a man who has undergone two separate physical examinations, one by Dr. Nichopoulos five days prior to his death, and another three weeks prior to his death by the doctor sent by Lloyds of London, and neither examination mentions the findings or diagnosis of "cardiac arrhythmia" when the Shelby County Medical Examiner claimed that the condition was severe enough to have killed him? What is the first thing that a doctor does when they examine a patient? Isn't it to pick up a stethoscope and listen to the patient's heartbeat? Clearly "arrhythmia" and other defects in the heartbeat can be detected simply and easily by carefully listening to the heart, so how did this diagnosis escape the notice of two separate doctors? The simple answer is that it didn't exist.

This more than explains the astonishment that Ulysses Jones had observed on Dr. Nick's face as he worked on Presley's body. Dr. Nick looked at Elvis in total disbelief, as if it were impossible that Elvis could be dead. Returning to the interview with Dr. Nick on *A Current Affair* on November 19th 1990, Nichopoulos says the following;

> *"I couldn't believe that he died. We didn't find anything that I might have messed up on or misdiagnosed, and if he had any heart disease we'd done treadmills, we'd done many cardiograms, and we had done things that should have alerted us that they was some problem here."*

Beyond the pushing and shoving over the autopsy verdict, this evidence alone calls the Shelby County Medical Examiner, Dr. Jerry T. Francisco a liar, but people don't just lie for the sake of lying. There is always a truth behind the lie is worth the cover up. Was Dr. Francisco lying by his own accord, was he being muscled, or simply told what to do?

This begs the question: who would want to murder Elvis, and how did they pull it off? Although his public life was as squeaky clean as ever, the last year of Presley's personal life was rife with infighting within the Memphis Mafia, and entanglements with both the FBI and the Mafia that were separate from Colonel Parker's gambling issues.

The continued drama from the pack of inane simpletons that surrounded this man would have been enough to drive any of us to the brink of insanity, and to make matters worse, everyone wanted something from him: Ginger wanted his money, fame and contacts, the Stanley boys wanted his drugs, Colonel Parker wanted to run every part of his life, Priscilla wanted her divorce settlement, the music critics wanted new material, Dr. Nick wanted loans for his business partnership, Joe Esposito and his business partners wanted money, and little Lisa Marie just wanted to see her daddy.

By the 1970s, Presley's personal staff at Graceland, including his expanded security detail, had grown to twenty and with more employees came more and more problems. Not only was this a fiscal nightmare for Elvis, but it became a personal one as well. Everyone turned to Elvis for something as they unloaded their personal and financial problems on him.

These people would have been enough to pull anyone apart. In reality, the only peace Elvis truly had in his life came from reading books on the world's religions and taking medicines.

While some of these medications were necessary to aid in the treatment of his minor health issues, others were *"downers"* so he could relax, relieve his insomnia and escape the horrible mess of problems that everyone dropped in his lap on an hourly basis.

Aside from his books and his sedated dalliances, Elvis had an interest in law enforcement and was very patriotic. He was a friend, and in some cases a fellow deputy, of law enforcement in literally every state. While seen as merely an entertainer to the public, there were behind the scenes meetings with President Nixon, as well as other governmental officials. Elvis knew that America was hurting, and he was eager to get involved.

The entertainment industry, as well as the country itself, was experiencing a hangover from the radical 60s as drug problems were lingering at all levels and the country was embroiled in anti-America rallies. Nixon, who'd become enormously unpopular due to the war in Vietnam, was quick to reward Elvis with a DEA badge, and he instantly worked as an undercover agent and drug informant for the FBI while doing his tours in Las Vegas.

So involved was Presley with the DEA and the FBI, that on the wall at Graceland there hangs a mounted letter from the FBI thanking Elvis for his *"cooperation."* After a great deal of investigation by Presley researcher Maria Columbus, it was revealed that Elvis had worked with the FBI to provide cover for their agents as bass players and backup singers in his band.

As these agents investigated the roots of the country's drug problem and other organized crime activities, it wasn't long before the underworld of Las Vegas and the mob were quickly informed of Presley's status as agent.

After all, here we have Elvis Presley staying at Mob-run hotels and casinos in Las Vegas, with Colonel Parker hobnobbing with mafia bosses and Elvis hiding federal agents assigned to investigate and to bust them. There is no way that this could end well.

If this wasn't enough to get a herd of cattle murdered, Elvis and his father had been involved in an FBI sting operation which began in 1976. Elvis, who was in the process of buying yet a bigger and more garish jet to keep up with his entertainment peers, was selling his older and smaller airplane, a JetStar, that he affectionately named Hound Dog II.

The JetStar was dry docked by the time Vernon had investigated Elvis' financial situation, and he quickly discovered that Elvis still owed $600,000 on a plane that he wasn't using. The plane was purchased for $899,702.60 on September 2nd 1975, and Vernon knew that selling the plane would help keep the Elvis solvent.

Vernon advertised the plane's sale, which attracted the interest of an underworld kingpin that the FBI had been watching internationally for nearly a decade. The kingpin told Vernon that he could lease the JetStar while making monthly payments back to the Presleys which would put Elvis' investment on the plane in the black. The conmen convinced Vernon to re-mortgage the plane for $950,000 for a lump sum of cash, which included the $600,000 to purchase the plane and $350,000 needed for renovations. Then, Vernon would accept their lump-sum payment for its purchase including and monthly installments until the plane was fully purchased. To this, Vernon agreed.

In the end, the newly-renovated plane vanished forever and all the checks that were written to Presley bounced. Inevitably, Presley was left holding worthless pieces of paper and he now owed more than double what the plane was originally worth.

The resulting complaint filed with the FBI put Elvis and his father directly in the middle of a case against the mob for racketeering and fraud. The following quote is from page 128 of John Parker's *Elvis: Murdered by The Mob:*

> *"Memo from FBI, Memphis division, to headquarters, 1977 To the Director, Federal Bureau of Investigation; Re: Elvis A. Presley (Victim); Investigation into this case predicated upon a request from the United States Attorney's office, Western District of Tennessee, Memphis, wherein they had been contacted by attorney for Elvis A. Presley, an entertainer, indicating they felt a violation of federal law had occurred...their client was the victim, losing approximately 950,000 dollars."*

By late July 1977, the FBI was ready to make arrests, with Elvis standing as a primary witness in the case against the mafia. Less than one month later, both Elvis, and the arrest warrants that had been served, were dead.

To expand upon the fact that Elvis was murdered we must return to the aforementioned television interview with Dr. Nick. Lost to history was the following quote from his 1990 interview. *"He could have had a broken neck or a concussion that I don't think would have been found at autopsy. I don't think x-rays were done, not in my presence."*

Is this possible? It is possible that the autopsy team started with what they thought was a cause of death and then worked backwards to try and fit it rather than explore all of the investigative avenues? Did the words "We think he OD'd" compromise the entire autopsy?

Apparently, the answer is yes, as Dan Warlick's notes and photographs of the death scene, which contained real evidence, were completely ignored by those in charge. Putting aside the autopsy team that was hyper focused on finding a drug death, it's time ask ourselves this very relevant question. Did someone in either in a calculated plot or a random fit of rage break Elvis Presley's neck?

Beyond question, as summer hit Memphis in 1977, there were more people who wanted Elvis Presley dead than alive, that much is well known. What isn't well known is who, or what set of circumstances combined to make that happen.

Grab your shovels, because it's time to do some serious digging into one of the greatest and most interesting cold cases in American history. It is time to investigate each suspect and answer the inevitable question - who murdered Elvis Presley?

4
The Suspects

> *"For whatever reason or motive, essentially no real effort was ever made to truly unearth the circumstances of Elvis Presley's death. It seems almost as if the city of Memphis itself does not care to know the truth about the death of its most prominent citizen."*
>
> -Geraldo Rivera, ABC News, 20/20, 1979-

Before we get into the pushing and shoving of who did what, it's important to understand the process that we must undertake to find the murderer.

When a crime is investigated, facts are gathered in an attempt to find those responsible so they can be brought before the courts and due process of the law can determine either their innocence or guilt.

That's how the American criminal justice system functions – at least in theory. When the facts are examined, criminal investigators put their personal feelings aside and follow the flow of the evidence to individuals who are called persons of interest.

A person of interest is a phrase used by law enforcement to announce the name of a person involved in their investigation but who has not been formally accused or charged with a crime.

In reality, a person of interest could be a witness, bystander, or someone whom law enforcement speaks with for the purpose of conducting the official investigation.

From there, detectives can screen and sift through witnesses and other persons of interest to find their suspects, and eventually make their arrests. This isn't an easy process, or a process based on speed – it's a process based on the methodical gathering and examination of facts.

This exacting process outlines three elements in the process of finding a suspect. The three elements are motive, means, and opportunity. Each suspect must have, within the findings of the crime, the motive, means, and opportunity to achieve the given result.

This three-element theory has proven so successful that it's now the primary foundation of crime-solving. According to a popular online dictionary, the definition for each of these terms are as follows:

Motive: something (as a need or desire) that causes a person to act.

Means: the medium, method or instrument used to obtain a result.

Opportunity: a favorable juncture of circumstances causing an action.

In the murder of Elvis Presley there were numerous persons of interest who should have been questioned, probed, and explored if indeed an official investigation into this suspicious death had transpired when Dan Warlick wanted it to.

Certainly everyone close to Elvis – especially his former wife Priscilla and his father Vernon –would have welcomed true answers to this very sudden and mysterious death.

In fact, Vernon Presley all but screamed for such an investigation from the day Elvis died until his own death two years later. Vernon's numerous requests and demands for a murder probe were totally ignored by the officials in the City of Memphis and the Shelby County District Attorney's office.

My question is, why? What did they have to hide? To add to this elongated mystery, most of these law-enforcement investigators and officials in high office were friends of Presley.

They aided him and his entourage in obtaining deputy badges at both the local and federal level, plus special pistol permits that allowed Elvis and his Memphis Mafia to carry concealed weapons legally as they flew from state to state while he was on tour.

It is impossible to imagine that not one of these officials could pull a string to have this final favor granted for Vernon. It is even more impossible to imagine that none of these officials would investigate this death to set the old man's mind at ease, especially with all the money and financial collateral Vernon would have been willing to pay. So, the raging question remains, why was no one compelled to investigate? Through each of their contacts, Elvis Presley and Tom Parker had managed to establish rich and personal friendships with three consecutive US presidents. Elvis had befriended both Richard Nixon and Jimmy Carter, and Tom Parker had befriended, and exchanged gifts with, Lyndon Johnson.

Yet, in the fourteen years these presidents collectively held high office in our nation, none of these 'commanders-in-chief', who oversee the entire US government, could command or motivate an investigation into this mysterious and sudden death?

Certainly, Colonel Parker with all of his numerous police contacts throughout the country – contacts made by arranging additional security in every state for Elvis – could have arranged to have a favor cashed in for a complete investigation.

How then, was it possible, or even remotely conceivable that Dan Warlick, under the direct supervision and command of his boss Jerry T. Francisco, could have closed the case on all these mysterious activities that he'd encountered without so much as ordering a coroner's inquest?

Elvis' death was ruled "due to natural causes" less than six hours after he'd been pronounced dead, and long before the autopsy evidence or the physical evidence Dan Warlick discovered at Graceland could be analyzed.

This is completely out of balance with logic. This is covered in Thompson and Cole's *The Death of Elvis* as they recount Warlick's actions. They write:

> "He (Warlick) picked up the phone and dialed the bureau. He reached the duty officer, Lieutenant G. E. Jordon, and reported that Francisco had preliminarily ruled that Elvis's death was a result of 'cardiac arrhythmia, causes unknown.' The Lieutenant asked if that meant Elvis died of natural causes. Warlick told him that was his understanding of what his boss had said. At that point, the Lieutenant jotted down "natural causes" and closed Memphis Police Department case No. 2793, the death of Elvis Aaron Presley."

It was never seen again, why? At 8:50pm on August 16th 1977, without having a single fingerprint lifted from Graceland, or without any investigation into the official facts by the homicide division, the case on the death of the biggest star the world had ever seen was freakishly and hastily closed.

This not only seemed impossible, but it also borders on illegal, as the two men acted in concert to perform such an act. In any court in the nation, the previous legal definition is a conspiracy, but before we go into any wild flights of fancy, why would Francisco, a very experienced and talented medical examiner, give such an obtuse order?

Who was behind it? What was their motive? To answer these questions, we must first ask many others. To begin, we must delve into this information and solve the first of the three elements of a crime: Motive. After all, people just don't kill other people without a motive, so that is the logical place to start.

There were numerous employees, girlfriends and hangers-on who were close to Elvis who had an 'axe to grind'. After years of research, I have compiled the following list of potential aggressors who had the motive to commit murder, and it's a good thing that I have, because in more than four decades no one else seemed to be very interested in doing so.

Keep in mind: Motive is the trickiest of the three necessary crime elements. Some motives generate fury, other motives are simple disappointments that eventually dissolve within a person and become lost over time.

Knowing this, it's important that we analyze each suspect closely to determine the root, and intensity behind his or her motivation. Below are persons of interest who had varied reasons to be motivated to murder. Let the investigation begin.

1. David Stanley
2. Ricky Stanley
3. Billy Stanley
4. Ginger Alden
5. Joe Esposito
6. Dr. George Nichopolous

7. Colonel Tom Parker
8. Delta Mae Biggs (Elvis' Aunt)
9. Billy Smith (Elvis' cousin)
10. Jo Smith (Billy Smith's wife)
11. Red West, Sonny West and Dave Hebler

I. MOTIVE

Motive: something (as a need or desire) that causes a person to act

David Stanley

While all the Stanley Boys (Billy, Ricky and David) grew up as Elvis' step brothers, and were raised at Graceland from young boys, David Stanley became one of the king's closest, and most trusted bodyguards.

As his responsibilities on the tours grew, necessity caused him to be an absentee husband and his young bride soon found comfort elsewhere. While Elvis worked to bring the couple back together, rumors that Elvis had seduced David's wife enraged him.

David soon viewed Elvis as the reason the couple was splitting and he set his sights on Elvis' girlfriend Ginger Alden. In fact, according to numerous reports, the last words that Elvis had spoken to his father were that David and Ginger were having an affair.

David's jealously over the alleged romance between Elvis and his ex-wife, combined with the alleged affair he was having with Ginger, created two powerful motives that became so obvious to Vernon that he asked David Stanley point blank if he had murdered Elvis. One account of Vernon's gruff accusation is featured in David Stanley's movie *Protecting the King*.

Ricky Stanley

Ricky Stanley, David Stanley's brother, was Elvis' stepbrother and personal valet the night he died. The bitter divorce that Vernon Presley and Dee (Stanley) Presley had undergone in 1977 weighed heavily on all three of Dee's boys. Ricky being the most sensitive of the brothers, was highly affected by the drama.

Billy Stanley

Billy Stanley was another of Elvis Presley's step brothers. He was especially upset with Elvis as he was rumored to have had a romantic affair with his wife. The fury went so far that Billy dropped all contact with Elvis and his Memphis Mafia, with the exception of his brothers.

From *The Death of Elvis*: *"Of the three, only Billy Stanley permanently deserted Elvis' fold. He became soured and disillusioned after discovering Elvis having an affair with his eighteen-year-old bride, Ann."*

Ginger Alden

Ginger was in awe of Elvis from the minute they met, but that soon wore thin. Ginger seemed to enjoy the notoriety of being known as Elvis' girlfriend more than actually being with him. She would eventually come and go as she pleased, in and out of local nightclubs, and preferred to stay at home with her mother then go on tours where Elvis needed companionship the most.

Elvis came to realize that she was after his money and was trying to use his many contacts to launch her own career in the entertainment industry. The couple fought often, especially in the week before Elvis died, as Ginger's sister discovered Elvis with another woman.

Her name was Alicia Kerwin, and when she visited Elvis, Ginger was so jealous that she would ring the phone off the wall. From the time Alicia and Elvis met, Ginger would try to intimidate her. They ran into each other while they were shopping, in traffic and even in night clubs. It was well known in Elvis' circle that he was in the process of dumping Ginger and desired to stop being her candy man. Shortly after Elvis died, a story emerged that no one close to Elvis believed – that Elvis had proposed marriage to Ginger.

This is hard to believe, as she claimed that he recycled a diamond from his TCB ring for her engagement ring. This makes no sense. If Elvis Presley, king of all things fancy and ornate, wanted to marry a woman, the diamond wouldn't be a second hand rock. It would have been the biggest and most ornate diamond in the state of Tennessee. To many, this story was specious.

It seemed that the notoriety of being Elvis Presley's fiancée was even greater after his death. Ginger succeeded in launching a successful acting career in TV commercials and soap operas. Hell hath no fury like a woman scorned, and her future stardom was in jeopardy of being taken away from her by another woman. Ginger was on the brink of losing everything, but was it a sufficient motive to murder?

Joe Esposito

Joe was one of Elvis' closest friends in the Army, and joined his full-time crew when he was discharged. As a very loyal and trustworthy friend, Esposito, like the other members of the Memphis Mafia, was given a pivotal job to keep the business going.

Esposito became Elvis' road manager and had enormous responsibility; however, as the years went by, Esposito became closer to Colonel Parker than Elvis, and actually became the Colonel's spy inside the Presley circle. Joe was a no-nonsense guy who had little time for the foolishness of drugs, canceled concerts or the impedances that the younger members of Presley's entourage brought.

Joe's focus was the business end of Presley and he wanted a smooth running show. This was the distinction he shared with Colonel Parker as the two men became a tight team. This is covered in numerous books, but none quite as thoroughly as in Nash's *The Colonel*: "In fact, since the May departure of Joe Esposito, the foreman of the entourage and the Colonel's chief spy, Parker couldn't even get his client on the phone."

In 1977, Esposito and a few investment partners were in the process of starting a string of racquetball courts using Elvis Presley's name. Elvis didn't object, and was always happy to help his friends. It blew up, however, when Parker got wind that Elvis' name would be in the public without his percentage.

Parker forced Elvis to withdraw from the deal leaving the other business partners, who'd invested a ton of money, to file a lawsuit against Elvis. The fury over the lawsuit was intense, but was it enough of a motive for Joe or his other business partners to commit murder? Was Joe Esposito friend or foe on August 16th 1977?

Dr. George Nichopoulos

Dr. Nick, also known to the Memphis Mafia as "Needle Nick", owed Elvis $275,000, and his practice was solely dependent on the Graceland crew for profits. This loan was done in proper legal fashion clearly showing signatures, dollar amounts, as well as the date.

This was as legal a contract as any that existed and one that Dr. Nick could have wanted out of. With Elvis Presley dead, the repayment of this note could have been called into question. This was indeed a motive to murder.

Colonel Tom Parker

Beginning in 1974, the once-famed relationship between Parker and Presley had again diminished, along with Presley's health. The men spoke mainly through middle men and avoided contact with each other if at all possible. As Presley battled a laundry list of ailments, from hypertension to an impacted colon, his weight ballooned and his energy level both onstage and in private life plummeted.

Elvis began to take on a sickly, bloated appearance that onlookers and critics ignorant to his illnesses, passed off as simply being "fat." These were the same ignorant people who started rumors of Elvis eating five dozen donuts and deep-fried peanut butter and banana sandwiches by the plateful. This was simply not the case. Elvis' illnesses were very real and his health caused him to cancel shows, and even leave the stage early if he was in discomfort.

To Tom Parker, by the mid 1970's, Elvis was becoming a bigger problem than he was worth. Aside from the obvious issues of the two men not getting along on a personal level, Presley's attendance at his shows was beginning to suffer. Less money in the door meant less money for Parker, and he wasn't happy. To Parker, Elvis wasn't holding up his end of the bargain, and to Elvis, Parker was trying to run every aspect of his life.

In fact, Parker wanted out so badly, that he tried to sell his end of the contract shortly before Presley's death. He was unsuccessful but would have done almost anything to sever the two. Did he murder Elvis?

Delta Mae Biggs (Elvis' Aunt)
Billy Smith (Elvis' cousin)
Jo Smith (Billy Smith's wife)
Billy Stanley, Ricky Stanley, David Stanley
The divorce between Vernon Presley, and his second wife, Davada Stanley, shortly before Elvis died in 1977 came at a high cost, and fallout for everyone at Graceland was disastrous. Legally, many things were done by Vernon's lawyer to safeguard his money and ensure it wouldn't involve Elvis, his bankroll or his estate in any way.

As one could imagine, this was a very involved and laborious deed for his attorney. As word of this split reverberated throughout the walls of Graceland, the Stanley boys were put in a very awkward position.

Their mother was getting divorced from Elvis' father, which was creating animosity, but their employer was Elvis himself. The friction was obvious.

To make matters worse, Vernon had now seized control of Elvis' books, and all of his financial decisions. As the year went on, rumors of more payroll cuts circulated, and with Vernon divorcing the Stanley boys' mother, the axe seemed imminent. But there was another problem.

For Vernon to totally rid the Presleys of Dee Stanley and her three boys, it would take more than firings and a simple divorce. The Stanley's were in Elvis Presley's will, along with half of his employees, and his extended family.

While Elvis was a very generous and giving man, Vernon could be vicious and he wanted everyone off the will with the exception of himself and Elvis' only true heir, Lisa Marie. There wasn't a day on this earth when Elvis didn't trust his "daddy", so when Vernon told his son this would protect him, Vernon quickly got his wish.

The following paragraph is the concluding excerpt of Elvis Presley's last will and testament, clearly showing the three witnesses sworn to sign and attest to the contents of the document.

"[Signed by Elvis A. Presley]
ELVIS A. PRESLEY

The foregoing instrument, consisting of this and eleven (11) preceding typewritten pages, was signed, sealed, published and declared by ELVIS A. PRESLEY, the Testator, to be his Last Will and Testament, in our presence, and we, at his request and in his presence and in the presence of each other, have hereunto subscribed our names as witnesses, this 3 day of March, 1977, at Memphis, Tennessee.

[Signed by Ginger Alden]
Ginger Alden residing at 4152 Royal Crest Place

[Signed by Charles F. Hodge]
Charles F. Hodge residing at 3764 Elvis Presley Blvd.

[Signed by Ann Dewey Smith]
Ann Dewey Smith residing at 2237 Court Avenue."

At Vernon's request, Elvis Presley's will was officially changed on March 3rd 1977. This seemed like a solid business move until the witnesses were chosen and learned what was going on. Witnesses included Charlie Hodge, Presley's stalwart confidant and Graceland resident and Ginger Alden.

When the word spread, Billy Smith, his wife Jo, his aunt Delta Mae as well as the Stanley boys flew into a rage. But for the Stanley brothers it was the final insult, and the last straw. Investigator Dan Warlick had long suspected that Jo and Billy Smith's account of Elvis' last night didn't add up, he had also noticed that the maids in Graceland looked to be afraid of Elvis' aunt, Delta Biggs. Did they all conspire to murder Elvis and hide the facts?

Red West, Sonny West, and Dave Hebler
In the wake of Priscilla's new divorce settlement, the new financial agreement with Colonel Parker (which was grossly unfair to Elvis), the lack of tax shelters and a huge payroll, Elvis was killing himself entertaining the masses resulting in his own personal poverty.

It wasn't known to anyone in Presley's entourage in 1976, but it was the year that Elvis nearly went bankrupt. This is how and why Vernon Presley took over Elvis' finances. In doing so, he frequently overextended his boundaries and acted without Elvis' permission.

The firing of longstanding bodyguards Red West, Sonny West and Dave Hebler was the vanguard of these times. The firing of these three men was a decision that Vernon should have skipped.

In a tasteless act, Vernon fired three of Elvis' most loyal and trusted bodyguards without warning, which created a tremendous amount of hard feelings – hard feelings that even Elvis couldn't smooth over in his many phone calls to the men offering large sums of money, and his help in finding them other jobs until he could employ them again.

Not believing that Elvis was in dire financial straits, or that Vernon had taken it upon himself to act without Elvis' permission, Elvis himself bore the full brunt of their vengeance.

Unwilling to accept Elvis' help or explanation, the men took the matter far more personally than professionally and set out to ruin Presley's name before the world. They soon teamed up with author Steve Dunleavey to collaborate on a "tattle-tale/tell-all" book, with the sole purpose of destroying the wholesome Presley name.

The book *Elvis, What Happened?* was published shortly before Elvis' death and included exaggerated stories with content that was neither truly sinister nor wholly damning. When Elvis got wind of the project, he was very hurt and offered the men anything they wanted to stop the book.

They refused and proceeded to punish Elvis for something that truly wasn't his fault. The book, known forever as *"the Bodyguard Book,"* was obviously published with revenge in mind. However, was there a motive for murder? Clearly the men all had vengeance at heart and acted in concert to sully Elvis' name for their own profit.

Each of these men were military trained and practicing black belts in karate. Any one of them could have killed Elvis with weapons or with their bare hands, and each had an axe to grind. In a gruesome twist of fate, after Elvis' death, their book soared to the best-sellers list as fans struggled to digest Presley's shocking and sudden death. How ironic. Was the motivation for their book to hit the best-sellers list incentive to murder Elvis?

SUMMARY OF MOTIVES

Clearly, each person of interest had a clear-cut motive, but whose motive was sufficient to enrage them to actually murder? Interestingly, everyone on the list, with the exception of Dr. Nick, had wrath and/or revenge as a catalyst for their motive. As we plug these same people into the second element of investigation, to establish means, the field will narrow.

II. Means

Means: the medium, method, or instrument used to obtain a result.

David Stanley

David Stanley certainly had the ability, method and instrument to kill. He joined Elvis and the other bodyguards in karate class where he quickly earned the nickname "headhunter."

The anger issues that David Stanley displayed during that time period were clearly depicted in his motion picture *Protecting the King,* which shows David getting out of hand with his newfound martial-arts skills and Elvis, ever the big brother, chewing him out.

Numerous times during the film David Stanley displays himself as a loose cannon suffering from a violent temper combined with a very serious drug problem. According to his movie, and apparently by his own admission, David went on to become so vicious with weapons and martial arts ability that he stepped up to replace Red West, Sonny West and Dave Hebler after they were discharged by Vernon.

Of the three Stanley brothers, David Stanley was by far the most lethal and possessed the worst temper. This isn't a good combination for a person of interest to have when they are involved in a murder investigation.

Ricky Stanley

Ricky Stanley was on duty as personal valet the night Elvis died and certainly had access to the wide array of drugs Dr. Nick had prescribed. Any of these drugs could have been forced down Elvis' throat while he was groggy, or crushed up and put in food to create a lethal drug overdose. Ricky Stanley admitted many times as the decades passed that he had a very serious drug addiction.

Both Joe Esposito and Sam Thompson recalled on many occasions that drugs prescribed for Elvis would often turn up missing at the hands of the Stanley boys. This is covered in *The Death of Elvis*: "*The Stanley brothers had a propensity for drugs and it is pretty evident that their taking of the drugs was so well known that Nick wouldn't let them have them. There was talk of Nick keeping his bag locked up for fear of them getting into it.*"

These quotes were relayed by Sam Thompson to the authors in an attempt to determine the whereabouts of the missing Stanley brothers. Ricky's alibi for not attending to Elvis or being present the night Presley died was drug-related: He recalled he was knocked out on downers. Although this is entirely possible, Ricky Stanley certainly had the ability, method and instrument to kill.

Billy Stanley

Billy Stanley had access to the whole of Graceland through his two brothers as well as access to the same drugs and weapons. Any or all of these could have been used by Stanley to murder Elvis and the evidence quickly and efficiently sanitized with the help of his brothers to escape detection. When examining the facts, no one can overlook Billy Stanley.

Ginger Alden

Without question, Ginger had the closest and longest access to Elvis, as she allegedly slept next to him the night he died. She could have done anything from feeding him poison, to forcing a secret drug overdose, to smothering him with a pillow while he lay in a drug induced and comatose state. When it comes to finding the one person with the most means to murder Elvis, the answer continues to be Ginger Alden. Without question, she had sole possession of the highest level of ability, method and instrument to murder.

Joe Esposito

Joe had a huge level of respect and responsibility within the Memphis Mafia and could have done practically anything within Graceland, and removed the evidence to cover his tracks without throwing up any red flags. He had equal access to Elvis' weapons, drugs, food, drinks and unlimited access to the man himself. Joe Esposito indeed had the ultimate backstage pass.

Dr. George Nichopolous

Dr. Nick, as he was known to the gang, was Presley's personal physician and cared for Elvis and his many health issues. He became accustomed to phone calls in the middle of the night jolting him out of bed, and was charged with prescribing, regulating and administering medication to Presley on a regular basis. Because he had access and control over Presley's drug intake, he remains on this list. Over-prescribing drugs certainly establishes the ability, method and instrument for murder.

Tom Parker

Beyond doubt, Parker had the means to kill. He also had the ability to have anyone killed as easily as putting the right word in the ear of any one of his mob ties, ties that dated back to the early 1940s. Not only did Parker possess personal access to Elvis anytime he wanted it, like Esposito, but he also had the influence over men who made people "disappear." The ability, method and instrument to murder Presley was very present for Parker.

Delta Mae Biggs, Billy Smith and Jo Smith

Although Elvis' aunt Delta Mae, his cousin Billy, and Billy's wife Jo could have been very upset when they learned that they'd been written out of Elvis' last will only weeks prior to his death, none of these people had the ability, method and instrument to murder Presley.

Delta Mae was in charge of Graceland's housekeeping staff, and had no normal access to anything that could really harm Elvis. She also had the maids on a very strict schedule and any deviation was impossible without directly sending up several red flags. Elvis' cousin Billy Smith, along with his wife, also lived on the Graceland grounds, but quite far back on the lot.

Even if they were upset about the will and had the desire to murder, they simply didn't have the ability, method and/or instrument to do so. Both Billy and his wife would have had such a long escape route going back to their house after the murder, they would have been seen on camera.

Billy was employed by Elvis in his security detail, and certainly wasn't telling the truth about the discovery of Elvis body, or its timeline but he, like his wife and Delta Mae benefited monetarily from a living, breathing Elvis.

Killing Elvis, even if they had good reason, wouldn't have been in their best interest to say nothing of the fact that their whereabouts was accounted for at the time of the murder. For these reasons Elvis' aunt, cousin and his wife are dropped as suspects in the murder of Elvis Presley.

Red West, Sonny West and Dave Hebler

Literally any one of these three men had not only the personal and physical training to murder, but they also had the connections to the mob, which could have allowed them to hire someone to kill Presley.

Combined with their knowledge of Graceland, the grounds, Elvis' personal habits and the natural cycle of business conducted prior to beginning a tour, they certainly could have been physically present to murder, or could have educated a hired killer to murder Presley.

Clearly, each of these spited enemies had the medium, method, or instrument to murder. If there were ever three men to pull out of the core of the Memphis Mafia, it should not have been these three.

Doubtless, if given the right motive, murder would have been the result by either singular, or combined efforts. There are two curious quotes from their book *Elvis, What Happened?* that define the level of influence and power that Presley, his manager and his bodyguards commanded within the Las Vegas Mob.

They reveal just how available professional killers were to anyone in the Presley sphere at any time. These quotes are in response to Elvis' wife leaving him for one of Elvis' friends and his desire to seek revenge. This quote is Elvis speaking to Red West.

> "Red, find someone, somebody to wipe him out. I want that sonofabitch dead...Make some calls...Find someone...I could find a hit man in ten seconds...You can do it, just do it."

Later in the book, Red explains the availability of professional hit men to Presley's circle and the rules that go along with the game.

> "In Las Vegas, you can get a telephone number for a strong-arm man fairly easily. The town was founded on that sort of thing. A mob hit can be organized from there for about five thousand dollars, although no hits are to be made in Vegas itself. That's Mafia policy."

The three men not only had the ability to kill Presley personally, they also had access to others who could kill for them remotely. In Presley's circle having the mob *"rub someone out"* would be that easy – especially for Red, Sonny and Dave.

SUMMARY OF MEANS

As expected, the list narrows. As we filter each person of interest through the second phase of the process, to determine who had the ability to commit the crime and the medium, method, or instrument used to obtain a result. Excluded from the investigation at this level are Elvis' Aunt, cousin and his cousin's wife, leaving all three of the Stanley brothers, Ginger Alden, Joe Esposito, Dr. Nick, Tom Parker and Elvis' three fired bodyguards to enter the third and last phase of the investigation, which is opportunity. As we continue the investigation, the field will again narrow to reveal the prime suspects in the case.

III. Opportunity

Opportunity: a favorable juncture of circumstances causing an action

David Stanley, Ricky Stanley, Billy Stanley and Ginger Alden

Ricky and David Stanley were at Graceland, and in Elvis' company within the 24-hour period prior to his murder. Also in Presley's company during that time period was Ginger Alden. Looking no further, this affords them the opportunity to commit murder.

Therefore, Ginger Alden, along with two of the three of the Stanley boys must stay on the list. Billy Stanley, on the other hand not only wasn't at Graceland during the timeframe in question, but he had removed himself from Presley's presence ages beforehand. Billy Stanley was nowhere around Elvis during the time period had no opportunity to murder him. Therefore, Billy Stanley needs to be removed from the investigation.

Joe Esposito

Joe arrived at Graceland the night prior to Presley's death and began work for the concert tour that was to begin the next day. Since he was present in Graceland during the time in question, complete with the motive and means to kill, he must graduate from the ranks of a person of interest to a murder suspect.

Dr. George Nichopolous

Dr. Nick wasn't near Graceland or Elvis within the 24 hours prior to Presley's death, thus to consider him a physical murder suspect would be impossible. To date, the only suspicious acts that Dr. Nick performed were to prescribe a mountain of medicine for the Memphis Mafia to share under the name of Elvis Presley, which threw up red flags and eventually cost him his medical license, and his refusal to turn over Presley's list of medicines to the EMTs when he was taken to the hospital.

Beyond these two issues, Dr. Nick went to great lengths to care for Elvis. It is also worthy to note that Dr. Nick supplied Elvis with a copy of the Physicians' Desk Reference to educate him, so an accidental overdose would be prevented. These aren't the acts of a murderer, and I've long thought that Dr. Nichopolous was far less than the hideous monster history has painted him. Since Dr. Nick didn't have the opportunity to murder, he must be dropped from the investigation.

Colonel Tom Parker

By every account, Tom Parker was in Portland, Oregon when he received the news that Presley was dead. Lamar Fike, Elvis' longtime friend and Memphis Mafia member, was with Colonel Parker in Oregon when he got the phone call. This should remove him as a suspect, but it doesn't.

The Colonel's fury over cancelled tours and Presley's drug habit, combined with his souring stage performances, put Parker in such a financial jam over his gambling debts that it would make him a very real threat.

When you add to the mix that Colonel Parker had access to a wide array of mob hit men and his right-hand man, Joe Esposito, was at Graceland in the 24-hour period of Presley's' death, Colonel Parker cannot be ruled out as a suspect.

The two men could have easily plotted to murder Presley as Esposito was equally fed up with Presley for both obvious and less-obvious reasons. For multiple reasons, Tom Parker must remain a person of interest.

Red West, Sonny West and Dave Hebler

These men aren't like Colonel Parker. They wouldn't have ordered Elvis to be killed – they would have killed him with their bare hands, but none were in the local area during in the 24-hour period of Elvis' death. None of the three men had the opportunity to murder. With a new book on the stands and regular public appearances to market their book project outside of the Memphis area, it is impossible to keep them on this list. Therefore Sonny, Red and Dave must be removed.

SUMMARY OF OPPORTUNITY

At this point in the investigation; Red West, Sonny West, Dave Hebler, Billy Stanley and Dr. George Nichopolous have all been released as persons of interest. None of them had the opportunity to murder Elvis Presley. As expected, the list narrows once again and reveals the five people who have met the final requirement. They are: David Stanley, Ricky Stanley, Joe Esposito, Tom Parker and Ginger Alden. All five of these people had the motive, means and opportunity to murder Elvis Presley, and all five of have been transformed from mere persons of interest into full blown murder suspects.

The fact that all five have passed all three of the elements of a crime has nothing to do with my personal opinion of these people. It has to do with the situation, as the night of August 15th became the morning of August 16th 1977. Nothing more. As an investigator of the situation, I am merely following where the facts of the matter lead me. It is now becoming clear that, beyond a shadow of a doubt, one of these five people murdered Elvis Presley.

EXAMINING THE SUSPECTS

All good investigators have one thing in common: they ignore their personal likes and dislikes and follow the evidence connecting the dots to solve the crime. This was a major stumbling block for Elvis' father; Vernon Presley, Elvis' Chief of Security; Dick Grob and Elvis' co-star (and my friend) Suzanna Leigh. All of these people are of the highest character and all of them were convinced that Elvis was murdered.

The problems that they had during each of their investigations were their personal likes and dislikes of the people surrounding Elvis. Their personal involvement with the people who were suspects, hampered their ability to objectively examine them. In other words they were too close to the situation to see it clearly. Because this was such a close group with such a vast mix of personalities within Graceland's staff, and in a city (Memphis) and county (Shelby) that didn't seem to care who or what killed Elvis, only an outside investigator could draw the necessary conclusions and find the murderer.

This is why my book is different than the others. I am an outsider. I am not part of their group, so my personal likes and dislikes won't hamper the investigation that you are about to take part in. Simply put: I don't care who killed this man, as long as we catch them. The investigation that is about to take place will be based solely on the evidence. I have split the field of the five murder suspects into two groups who could have acted in concert to murder.

Group 1
David Stanley, Ricky Stanley, and Ginger Alden

Group 2
Joe Esposito and Colonel Tom Parker

Group One Analysis

As we examine Group 1 (Stanley, Stanley, and Alden), we can link their circumstances together and hypothesize how the murder occurred. When Elvis told his father, shortly before his death, about his suspicion that Ginger was having an affair with David Stanley, he was correct. For Ginger, the choice was an obvious one to make. To be romanced by a young handsome man was certainly more befitting a young, gorgeous woman like Ginger than sleeping next to a pudgy, middle-aged, comatose man who was rumored to be impotent towards the end of his life.

To set the scene, on August 16th 1977, sometime after Presley slipped into his nightly drug-induced coma, Ginger left Graceland, dolled herself up and went to party with the Stanley boys. Who could blame them or her? It was a hot summer night, the town was abuzz with action, and their twenty-something hormones were raging. It has also been widely reported that Ginger would often leave Elvis to go out on the town, and Elvis would commission David Stanley to keep tabs on her. The two obviously met away from Graceland and started a secret affair that Presley got wind of.

Ginger Alden's disappearance more than explains Dick Grob's three nagging questions during his investigation. In Grob's book, *The Elvis Conspiracy*, he ponders the following: 1.) Why Ginger was so "dolled up" when the body was discovered; 2.) Why it been so many hours before Elvis' corpse was found, as the condition of his corpse revealed; and 3.) Who called and tipped off the media before the EMTs were called?

Each of these nagging questions could have only been answered by a group of people returning from a night of partying, to make a gruesome discovery. In truth, none of the Stanley brothers or Ginger Alden were present the night Presley was murdered, or the murder couldn't have happened.

By their own admission, the Stanley boys were partying at a local motel instead of doing their jobs the night that Elvis died, and unfortunately, Ginger Alden and most likely her sister were with them. Shortly after Elvis was knocked unconscious from his nightly drug ingestion, Ginger left to find excitement elsewhere.

A Fox News article published on November 20, 2010 entitled *The King and I: Travels with Elvis' Stepbrother* indicates that very thing. The article continues:

> *"But according to Dick Grob, Elvis' chief of security, David Stanley admitted that he and his brother had been partying with women all night at a nearby motel, and were passed out when Elvis died. Elvis' personal physician, George Nichopoulos, "Dr. Nick," repeated the allegations in his own book."*

Vernon Presley wasn't buying David Stanley's story either, and continued to question both David and Ginger separately. As described in Nash's *The Colonel*, Vernon Presley confronted Ginger:

> *"She (Ginger Alden) would be questioned later about why it took so long to discover Elvis. How was it that he had lain unattended in the bathroom floor for perhaps three hours or more? Was it possible that someone had come into the room that morning, someone that she did not perhaps recognize, perhaps? Vernon Presley asked her that very question. It was possible, she would say, because she was sleeping so soundly."*

In reality, she couldn't have answered this question or any question properly because she wasn't there. She also had the timeline of Elvis' discovery wrong before she called downstairs for help. As described in *The Death of Elvis*, she tells investigator Dan Warlick:

> *"Between 1:00 and 1:30 pm she said she woke up again. Still no Elvis. This time she went to the bathroom, found the body and called downstairs. Thus Ginger's estimate of when she found Elvis' body was thirty minutes to one hour earlier than the 2:00 p.m. distress call Al Strada mentioned."*

It's also odd that the two accused of having an affair – Ginger Alden and David Stanley – were mysteriously absent the night Elvis died, but oddly present when the body was discovered, all of which caused some very interesting reactions. For example: Who was it that David Stanley tossed in his Datsun 240Z before he raced past Sam Thompson to get off Graceland's property before the authorities arrived?

The cloaked passenger was slouching down in the seat and witnesses couldn't tell if it was a man or a woman, but one question must be asked; why was getting this mystery person out of Graceland suddenly more important than his dead stepbrother? There is no good answer to this mental wrestling match because the question far outweighs any possible answer that could be given. This ever changing and baffling story has been well documented in several books, but none as well-written as John Parker's *Elvis, Murdered by the Mob*. There he explains the event:

"David Stanley said he was playing pool with a friend when he heard the news. His first thought was to get his friend, who he had admitted later should not have been at the house, out of the gates as quickly as he could. It was a curious thing to do, at such a time, when his beloved stepbrother and provider was lying dead on the floor. He put his friend in the car and drove towards the music gates, just as the ambulance swung into the driveway. Stanley came back a few minutes later, entering the house through the rear, and bounded up the service stairs to Elvis' bedroom."

This begs many obvious questions: was David Stanley helping the murderer escape? Did David Stanley know the murderer well enough to alter the crime scene?

Was he in on the murder? Was he the murderer? Was he an accomplice to the murder, or was he just a bystander on the downside of an all-night drunken binge acting erratically?

Since the Stanley brothers and the Alden sisters all had legitimate bones to pick with Elvis, they could have been plotting to murder him in the morning when they returned to Graceland.

This is entirely possible, since the time of Presley's death was medically determined to be 9:00am More of the pieces of the puzzle begin to fit when we realize the toxic mixture of information that would have been revealed within this group of people.

The Stanley boys already had obvious reasons to be upset with the Presley family. The bitter divorce between their mother and Vernon was getting nastier with each passing day, and they apparently believed the rumor that Elvis had romanced David Stanley's wife. Anger, jealousy, revenge – take your pick. Each and every one of them was certainly driving force to murder.

These bones of contention were indeed causing widespread hostility, but there were two bits of information that only Ginger Alden knew that would have thrown every one of the Stanley boys into a full-blown, drug-induced, murderous rage.

Ginger, knowing that her days with Presley were numbered because he was replacing her with another woman, would spare no detail in fueling the fire of the Stanley boys to the fullest by informing them that she was a witness that signed the Stanley boys out of Presley's last will, and had recently overheard Elvis say that people weren't doing their jobs and that more employee changes were coming.

Those changes would have involved eliminating the Stanley brothers from the Presley payroll, as well as his life entirely. Elvis knew that changes needed to be made and he was ready to make them.

From replacing his manager, to his employees, all the way down to his girlfriend – and he was ready to make them. When one examines the connection of motive, means and opportunity for the two people who acted the most erratically on the day Presley was discovered, it's impossible to move past Ginger Alden being *"made up like she was going to a mannequin parade"* as Dick Grob put it, or David Stanley racing a mystery person out of Graceland at a high rate of speed.

If you play the scene out in your mind you could imagine the Stanley boys accompanied by Ginger Alden sneaking back into Graceland, desperately trying not to let on that they'd been absent. After assembling around the pool table, an argument erupts when Ginger spills the beans about the will and their jobs getting the axe.

The Stanley boys, no doubt lead by David, march upstairs to confront Elvis about what they heard and a violent altercation erupts where one of the Stanley's – all of whom have brutal tempers and were trained in martial arts – strikes Elvis and breaks his neck. The broken-neck theory coincides perfectly with what Dr. Nick had reported as Presley's true cause of death.

After a brief *"Oh my God, what do we do now?"* meeting, Ginger calls her mother at work who calms her down and tells her that she could profit from the death by calling an exclusive story into a reporter. This phone call is well documented and satisfies Ginger's desire for a claim to fame.

Dick Grob claimed that Ginger had called James Kirk, the National Enquirer contact in Memphis, on the very morning that Elvis died long before she alerted anyone about Presley's condition. Kirk received the call at around 11amand the voice was very familiar to him as he had spoken to Ginger on many occasions. If this is true, Ginger began to peddle her story for profit, hours before calling for help. Dick Grob in his book *The Elvis Conspiracy* writes:

> "He believed it was Ginger. He had talked to her several times before. The caller, Kirk said, instructed him to come to Graceland, saying 'that something was going on.' A second phone call, Kirk said, came in at 2:00 pm from the same woman, who ordered him 'to come at once and bring money.' Kirk said he had arranged with The Enquirer to pay Ginger $105,000 for her exclusive story."

Grob wrote that he investigated further to see if he could find some circumstantial evidence to verify Kirk's account. He claimed to have found it in interviews with Joe Esposito, Al Strada, and Charlie Hodge – all of whom reported that Ginger looked fresh, all showered, dressed and made up, when they raced upstairs.

Grob also learned from two maids on duty, that they heard the shower running upstairs at a time when Elvis must have been unconscious on the bathroom floor. Asking why Ginger would be so disloyal to Elvis, Grob said that obviously the answer was money.

Grob said Elvis had no real intention of marrying Ginger and that she knew it. Adding the fiction to the story, that she was his fiancée catapulted her to instant stardom, and she capitalized on what had happened. The Stanley boys, on the other hand, had a far bigger problem: how could they explain away what had happened? As time passed and they worked on their stories, they were shocked to learn that the EMTs were coming, and if Elvis wasn't really dead, he could tell what had happened? Was Billy Stanley at Graceland and was he with his brother when he attacked Elvis? If so he certainly didn't belong there as he was no friend of Elvis Presley's at the time of his death. That would, however, explain who David's mystery passenger was that he raced off Graceland's property. Was it Billy Stanley that David tossed in his Datsun 240Z, telling him to hunch down, as he raced his brother to safety?

I could imagine a situation where, in their nervousness, they pick up the drug packets that had fallen out of their pocket during the scuffle with the large and drugged Presley. This more than explains why the death scene appeared "*messy*" to Dan Warlick – as if a struggle had taken place. As the day wears on, the Stanley's sedate themselves to relieve their nerves, and when they come down off of their high, the announcement of a heart attack is made to cover the murder.

Ironically Dr. Nick, Ginger and Vernon all surprisingly blurted out that Elvis was murdered and all three of these people mentioned and/or questioned David Stanley of the deed. One could even go on to hypothesize that the guilt that the Stanley brothers felt, regarding the murder, drove them to the ministry of Jesus Christ, where their nerves and their souls would both be saved. Amazingly, all of the Stanley brothers would go on to be involved, at various levels, with religion. In fact, in the years that followed, Ricky Stanley would go on to minister his own church.

Group Two Analysis

Although Elvis Presley signed the paychecks, Tom Parker was Joe Esposito's boss and Joe never made a move without him. Joe Esposito was a dutiful employee in every sense of the word. He was also Parker's puppet, spy and personal extension when he wasn't a welcomed guest of Presley.

When Parker wanted something done, he always knew he could put Joe on the job and it would be done completely and totally to his satisfaction. Joe was levelheaded, intelligent, responsible, and reliable in every sense of the word. He was also widely known as Parker's number-one snitch and mouthpiece. When Elvis' tours started, the 24-hour-men would leave a day ahead of time to set everything up. This crew usually consisted of Tom Parker, Lamar Fike, Sonny West and a few others.

Joe, on the other hand, was left behind to help ready the equipment with people like Al Strada, Charlie Hodge and, at times, the Stanley boys. Because both the in-town, and out-of-town crews needed to work and coordinate themselves perfectly, it was always Joe Esposito and Tom Parker who burned up the phone lines to achieve perfect synergy. Because of their positions with the tour, the two men saw each other more than their wives and would eventually become closer to each other than they ever were to Elvis.

When things went well, it made for the smoothest-running show in history complete with four jets and twenty-one tractor trailers full of equipment. But when Elvis was sick or had to cancel tours, it was a nightmare on the two men. By the mid-1970s, as Presley's illnesses and moods often collided, the two men often found themselves frequently at odds with their employer.

The situation worsened greatly when Parker and Elvis hadn't spoken directly in two years, and Parker formed Boxcar Enterprises to merchandise Presley's image and name. When this happened, Elvis Presley the man became of little worth to Parker, who could make more money selling posters and trinkets.

Parker excelled at merchandising since the 1940's, when he managed Eddy Arnold so forming that type of business was an obvious fit. Boxcar, which was formed in 1974, provided Parker with another way to pay off his gambling debts whether Presley was dead or alive.

It wasn't long before Elvis became a worthless cog in the Parker's merchandising machine and he wanted him out of the way. Joe Esposito was equally unhappy with Presley due to concert changes, plus his involvement in a lawsuit against him.

That's right: Joe Esposito, the best man at Presley's wedding, employee, and longtime friend, was actually suing Elvis over a failed real-estate venture along with his investors! With Parker and Esposito as personally close as they were, and with equal access to Elvis, Graceland, and his drug supply during the 24-hour period before Presley's death, it wouldn't have been a far stretch for these men to coordinate the murder and remember that Esposito's story of Elvis' death kept changing.

As Dan Warlick noted during his investigation, like David Stanley, Esposito was so good at telling everyone the truth that he told it many different ways. This begs the obvious question: was Joe covering up for the murderer, was he the murderer himself, or was Colonel Parker changing his story for him?

With both Esposito and Parker equally upset with Presley, they could have put their heads together and hatched a scheme to murder Elvis, that would result in an undetectable and natural-appearing death. Oddly enough, this is exactly what the death was ruled.

Playing out this scenario of murder, Joe Esposito easily could have arrived at Graceland prior to Elvis leaving for his 10:00pm dentist appointment. While Elvis, his daughter, and Ginger were out, Esposito could have passed unnoticed upstairs to Elvis' private suite and slipped an undetectable poison into his water glass, knowing that Elvis would indulge in his nightly routine of pills.

The end result of the Esposito/Parker murder would have made Parker a millionaire many times over – a situation he desperately needed to cover his bloated and growing gambling debts. But Esposito? What was in it for Joe?

Beyond his disgust with the additional work that cancelled concert dates demanded, and his lawsuit against Presley based on a failed real-estate venture, how did murdering Elvis Presley really benefit him? Naturally Joe was hostile toward Presley and fed up with every situation involved, but would he indulge Colonel Parker in committing murder? How would it benefit him? Money? Hardly, Joe Esposito was Elvis' highest-paid employee who raked in a hefty forty thousand dollars a year (a king's ransom in 1977). Would Parker strike a deal with Esposito for a portion of the take? That too was unlikely, as Parker already had a partner to monetarily satisfy.

So it's unlikely Esposito would have been easily bought, nor was the murder rap worth losing the payroll. So where's the motivation? With Elvis alive, Joe had steady employment and a chance that the lawsuit he got sucked into, would be settled out of court for a lump sum of cash.

With Elvis dead, Joe wouldn't have had the opportunity at either of these things, so it stands to reason that Joe Esposito, like Dr. Nichopoulos, would have benefited financially from Elvis being alive rather than dead. Even though Esposito had successfully passed through all three elements of the crime – motive, means and opportunity – it would be simply illogical, and against his best interest for him to murder Presley.

Therefore, Joe Esposito must be dropped from this investigation along with the Stanley brothers. Although they weren't thrilled with the idea of Vernon and their mother putting them in the middle of a nasty divorce, and they had many bones to pick with Elvis on frivolous issues they all benefited more from Elvis alive than dead.

For starters, they all loved the drugs they continuously pilfered from his black bag. Eliminating Elvis would mean eliminating their drug source, which at their level of dependency, would have been an unwanted thing to do. Furthermore, they also loved the excitement and the women that came along with being around Elvis as he toured the country.

Although the role they played in the actual running of things has been greatly exaggerated in recent years from the errand bots and peons they actually were, they would have been fools to kill the golden goose who delivered not only their drugs, but their paychecks as well.

Of the three Stanley brothers, David Stanley, with his martial arts and weapons training, horrid temper, divorce issues and daily access to Elvis would be of the greatest threat to harm Presley. These factors combined with the mystery person that he hastily raced off the grounds when the body was discovered, the cover-up of the death scene that he admitted to in later years, would seem to lead to many suspicious conclusions.

I agree. I also agree that all of it begs further investigation, especially when the identity of this mystery person continues to change with each passing decade. However, we must bear in mind that the murderer had enough pull in local government and law enforcement to have Dan Warlick's investigative findings ignored, and the case conveniently closed by the medical examiner before it ever began.

This is exactly what happened when the homicide division was called off and Presley's death was ruled natural causes, before the autopsy had even started. The fact that someone had enough pull in

Francisco's office to have him ignore standard protocols, such as a coroner's inquest, was more than just coincidence – it was planning.

Although David Stanley's suspicious behavior begs a more in-depth look, none of the Stanley brothers had this level of pull within the City of Memphis or Shelby County, Tennessee. For them to pull off the murder in this capacity, and orchestrate the cover-up, would have been virtually impossible.

Also, the preplanning and timing required to murder Elvis Presley would have had to been perfect. The murderer had to know the exact window of opportunity to strike – immediately prior to the start of a tour when the majority of Elvis' personnel were away from Graceland. They also would have known Elvis' daily routine and been able to pick the perfect time of day to enter undetected.

The knowledge that Ginger and David Stanley were having an affair, and that she was absent was also a key to gaining access, as was the fact that Presley's personal valet would have been absent as well. There was also the additional knowledge that three of Presley's meanest and deadliest bodyguards had recently departed, which left a very serious security hole. In the assassin's line of work there's no room for surprises, miscalculations, or haste.

Professional assassins never rush. They plot and plan every minor detail to the most minor degree. It's highly unlikely that this perfect murder could have been orchestrated by a man, who rushed a person out of Graceland in his car, at entirely the wrong time and was seen by everyone. Murdering a famous person is one thing, getting away with it is quite something else. Ginger Alden was a Memphis belle with many ties to local government. Her mother, Jo Alden, was an employee at the Internal Revenue Service and her father, Walter Alden, was a career military man who was ironically in charge of the public-relations fiasco at Presley's military induction ceremony in 1958.

Pictured is Walter Alden with Elvis at his military induction

Ginger, who also had the motive, means, and opportunity to murder Presley, would have easily known the ins and outs of everything necessary to plot, plan and either kill Presley herself or hire the hit and supply the murderer with all the information to complete the task.

Remember that Elvis didn't take to just any girl. He liked his woman to have both beauty and brains, and this gorgeous brunette hit the jackpot on both. Without a doubt, if she was to plot Elvis' murder, she would have been cunning enough to pull it off, but was her stumbling block the same as the Stanley brothers'?

Did she have deep and ready access to the proper levels of government that could have forced Jerry Francisco to ignore Dan Warlick's evidence, have the death ruled natural causes and call off a homicide investigation even before the autopsy started?

While bearing in mind those questions, let's explore another: If every part of the murderer's timeline was meticulously planned far in advance, as all professional assassinations are, how would we explain Ginger Alden's clumsy attempt to profit off the story by calling a local reporter?

These erratic actions, much like David Stanley's frantic automotive ejection of a person from Graceland's property in the midst of Presley's death discovery, simply would not have happened if either of them were in on the murder.

Assassinations are planned out like clockwork and every tiny problem or detail that could possibly be thrown into the mix would be managed far in advance. Like the Stanley's, Ginger simply didn't have the clout to make the medical examiner break from his professional protocols, or the cool demeanor, at the necessary time to be involved.

Therefore, this investigation can also remove Ginger Alden from being involved in Elvis Presley's murder. In truth, the only thing Ginger did wrong was to leave Presley's comatose bedside to go party, and return to clumsily try to profit from her gruesome discovery. Profiting from the Elvis Presley name was apparently a family trait for the Alden's.

Ginger's mother unsuccessfully sued the Presley estate for nearly forty thousand dollars immediately following Presley's death, claiming that Elvis had promised to pay off her mortgage. This wouldn't have been a surprise to anyone, as Elvis had impulsively purchased many homes for his friends, including his longtime friend Jerry Schilling.

However, if Elvis had indeed planned to do this, it would have been done as a surprise because Elvis never promised gifts. This alone indicated his intentions to abandon Ginger, along with her family. Ginger's account of their engagement was also suspect – the ring he gave her was a recycled diamond from his TCB ring.

In a 1980 interview with Ginger Alden, she said: *"The ring came from Elvis's TCB ring, which he always wore on stage. It was a large ring with lightning bolts down the side, and I believe it was in black onyx, and Elvis had a jeweler Lowell Hayes take the diamond from that ring and put to this (ring)."*

If Elvis had indeed given anyone an engagement ring, it would have been among the most ornate and gaudy diamonds on record, not a recycled one. Ginger never wanted Elvis; she just wanted to use his money and his contacts as her personal stepping stone to launch her career, and her fabrication of the engagement story was all part of it.

This is well covered in a book co-authored by Marty Lacker's wife, Patsy, entitled *Elvis: Portrait of a Friend*. Patsy writes that during Elvis' funeral service

Ginger sat with a mirror in her hand, fixing her hair and eyelashes. She further writes that Presley's entourage took offense to Ginger's mother at the cemetery after the funeral service, as they saw her standing outside of the mausoleum pointing out celebrities to Ginger and treating the solemn occasion as nothing more than an opportunity for Ginger to be seen and ultimately, discovered.

In reality, Ginger Alden was not a bad person then, and is not a bad person now. She wasn't a murderer. She was just a vain, self-centered little girl in a woman's body. It would have been impossible for Ginger to love anything more than herself in 1977, and the fact that she brought her most prized possession to the funeral, a mirror, speaks volumes.

The Aldens were in good company as they tried to monetarily level jump and glom off of Elvis' star power for their fortune. It didn't make them bad people. It's just the way it was. It was a common occurrence. In fact, almost everyone directly profited from Presley's stage show as their lone cash cow.

The operative words in this paragraph are "almost everyone". Only one person had the foresight to rearrange their profit structure away from a living Elvis Presley and they would profit tremendously from his murder. Incredibly, it's the same person who had the contacts to make the murder happen and make it all look like an accident. They also had the public relations contacts and political clout at the highest levels to cover it all up and spin it anyway they wanted. *Mox ut reveletur.*

5
The Rabbit Hole

> *"I told Vernon that I was sound asleep and had seen nothing. He asked me if it was possible that anyone had come into the bedroom while Elvis and I were asleep. He was talking about foul play - I could not rule it out."*
>
> *- Ginger Alden, The Death of Elvis-*

Immediately after the news of Elvis Presley's death rang in the ears of the world, millions of dollars were made selling records, tee-shirts, posters and other forms of merchandising.

Presley's unexpected demise made a ton of money before his corpse was even in the ground, and who stood behind the cash register with fists full of cash? Tom Parker.

Tom Parker is the only suspect in the murder investigation who didn't need Elvis Presley alive to make his fortune. Parker had removed himself from that dependency years earlier with the 1974 establishment of Boxcar Enterprises. In fact, to Parker, a living Elvis was a detriment.

With the murder of Elvis Presley, Tom Parker singlehandedly managed to outsmart and out maneuver the entire Presley family, Elvis' estate, most of their attorneys and make a fortune in the process.

Boxcar Enterprises made its fortune from Elvis' image, which never tires, never fights or argues with its management, never takes breaks between tours, never involves itself with the law enforcement affairs of the federal government, never pissed off the Mafia, and never cancels concerts due to illness.

Once Elvis Presley stopped being seen as a man and started be seen as a business with an international brand, the man himself became expendable.

Elvis' image was far easier to manage than Elvis himself. The man as his image can be plastered on anything, 24-hours-a-day, and it always makes money, money that Parker desperately needed. Whoever coined the phrase necessity is the mother of invention knew exactly what they were taking about, especially in this situation.

Tom Parker was so far ahead of the game that his vision of making a fortune from Elvis' image, memorabilia, and record sales the was the precursor to Elvis Presley Enterprises. Today, expanding on Parker's vision, EPE manages does far more than just manage the operation of Graceland.

It also manages the worldwide licensing of Elvis-related products, the development of Elvis-related music, film, video, television, stage productions, the ongoing development of Elvis' internet presence, and the management of all Presley's music publishing.

In today's world if you see anything with Elvis Presley's name, image, or voice attached, EPE is behind it ringing the cash register, and the idea came from none other than Tom Parker. After Presley's death in 1977, Parker was still entitled to 50% of Elvis' income, after taxes, which was the equivalent of financial sodomy.

After Vernon Presley died of a broken heart in 1979, the cost of running the Elvis estate, which included Graceland, exceeded half a million dollars annually, and with Parker reaping the greatest portion of the profits, it wasn't long before Parker and Presley's estate found themselves at odds.

By the time the 1980's rolled around, the two sides were embroiled in a very heated legal battle as the IRS was demanding almost $15 million in taxes from Elvis' estate, an estate that teetered on the brink of bankruptcy.

Eventually the court ruled in favor of the Presley family but only after a long and ugly court battle resulting in Parker countersuing. The countersuit was eventually settled out of court for a handsome lump sum of cash.

The dollar value was never made public but one of my contacts close to the situation revealed the staggering amount. Needless to say, Tom Parker, once again, had managed to outsmart everyone. The Presley estate finally came to realize what Parker knew all along, and they spent a fortune wrestling it out of Parker's hands.

Parker was a shrewd old soul. He didn't just saunter into Presley's personal suite and murder him. That would be far too traceable, obvious and clumsy for a man with so many high-profile Mafia contacts. It would also be uncharacteristic of a man who had always exercised great vision, wisdom, and foresight, and as the Presley estate eventually discovered, he was never clumsy or bumbling in anything he did.

It wasn't until I began doing research for this book and made contact with some of Elvis' friends that I began to realize what a tyrannical megalomaniac Tom Parker really was. The first person I had a telephone conversation with was a man named Paul Lichter. Lichter was not only one of Presley's personal friends, but he is also the owner of the Elvis Unique Record Club.

Paul had many business dealings with Parker before, during, and after Presley's death, and recalled Tom Parker as:

> "... *so smart, that talking to him was like talking to an entire encyclopedia. He was difficult to deal with sometimes because he was so far ahead of whatever anyone was thinking. He was the kind of guy who could carry on two or even three trains of thought at one time. He was always thinking and had everything figured out ahead of time.*"

Apparently Paul knew in advance what everyone else would find out years later. While everyone in the world was focused on Elvis Presley and his electric magnetism, they almost totally ignored the man behind him who could move worlds with one ten-second phone call. Parker was the perfect person to overlook. He was oafish and awkward and was certainly no one the camera would waste time on.

Unidentified photo: www.tapatalk.com

His pudgy stature and boyish face appeared to disarm casual observers, which allowed this plotting genius to hide in plain sight. On first appearance, no one would ever guess that he was every bit the scam artist P.T. Barnum was. Nor could they guess how deep his personal rabbit hole went.

No one would have ever guessed that he was a murdering stowaway who entered the United States illegally, on the run from the law. Besides, Tom Parker, or Andreas van Kuijk as he was known in the Netherlands (the country of his birth) had learned a lot since he narrowly escaped prosecution for bludgeoning a young woman to death on the eve of his escape to America.

As history tells us, this wouldn't be the first time Parker would have to plan his way out of trouble to achieve his ultimate prize. How deep does the rabbit hole go? Deeper than anyone had possibly imagined.

Andreas van Kuijk grew up in the small town of Breda. At a young age he became fascinated with carnivals and would eventually run away from home to join the circus. It was there that he learned the trade that would serve him the rest of his life.

Andreas, or "Dreis" as his siblings called him, started working the lowest and most menial of jobs the circus had to offer, quickly excelled and was given more responsibility. Alanna Nash in *The Colonel* writes:

> *"Before long, he was working shoulder to shoulder with the principals, first as a circus water boy – following along after clowns and smoking the butts of the cigars they threw on the ground – then as a feeder and caretaker of animals."*

As Dreis perfected his carnival skills, he longed to make it to America, and worked in the local shipping docks where he stashed away as much cash as possible for his future voyage.

That was the plan until May of 1929 when he vanished into thin air, leaving behind a pile of money and all of his worldly goods. Questions about his quick and hasty disappearance remained a forgotten mystery to those who noticed that he was gone at all, and for the next fifty years his family would be left with only an occasional photo that he mailed them, which generated more questions than answers.

The family pondered endlessly over the decades why Dreis, who'd always loved material things, would run off and leave his fancy clothes, gifts and even a large sum of cash. His family tried very hard to make sense of the happenings but could never make their many theories work.

He wasn't sick or dead, and he obviously wasn't mad at anyone in the family, because he'd send photos and even write short sentences to let them know that he was alive and well. The family was tormented by this ongoing puzzle, and as the decades rolled by both of his parents went to their graves unable to unlock the mystery.

Eventually fate would intervene and provide the answer to author Alanna Nash. It was the May 17th 1929 when Andreas van Kuijk ceased to exist in Breda and the person known as Tom Parker was created in the United States of America.

It was also the day that a brutal murder of a young woman, Anna van den Enden, was discovered. Anna was a newlywed. She was the wife of a storekeeper in Breda and she knew the Van Kuijk family well from their meetings at various church gatherings. Her husband shared Dreis' fondness for the circus and would travel great distances to participate whenever possible.

Dries and Anna's husband were good friends, which made the discovery of her murder at Dries' hands even more baffling. At some point during this mysterious encounter he took a blunt object and bashed Anna in the back of the head, killing her. Alanna Nash in her book *The Colonel* writes: *"...she was struck several times from behind and hit with such force that, as the police report vividly put it, "part of her brain came through the right ear."*

The local police who continued to investigate the crime questioned many people but none of the information that they were able to gather created any leads. For months they continued to ponder why a women who had no enemies would be so violently murdered. They were also unable to determine why her body, as well as the entire crime scene, was sprinkled with pepper.

In 1929, only a person who had worked with dogs would know of their uncanny ability to be used by European countries to sniff out clues and help solve crimes. Andreas van Kuijk, a caretaker of animals in the circus, would have learned this very early in life. Pepper would provide the perfect cover to make the dogs sneeze so much that they couldn't do their blood hounding duties or aid in solving the crime – a crime that would never be solved.

The stall tactic afforded Dries the time necessary to stow away in the hold of a ship bound for America. Once off the ship, on the other side of the world, he would be able to blend in with the masses and escape criminal prosecution. It was the perfect plan.

Technology was decades off from linking every fiber optic impulse across the world, and the primitive law enforcement techniques of the day were insufficient to track anyone down over such distances.

It was due to careful planning, cunning, and a little bit of luck that on the night of May 17th 1929 Andreas van Kuijk would forever vanish into the ocean fog and Tom Parker would emerge on the other side a free man.

More than half a century later two co-workers named Lamar Fike and Byron Raphael were made aware of Parker's murderous past, and were interviewed about his violent personality traits.

Fike, one of Presley's high school friends and a member of the Memphis Mafia, was assigned to work with Parker in readying concert locations days in advance. He was part of the previously mentioned 24 hour team. When asked about the Colonel, Lamar told Nash:

> "I don't think there's any doubt that he killed that woman. He had a terrible temper. He and I got into some violent, violent fights. We fought all the time."

Byron Raphael, the Colonel's assistant at the Phillip Morris Agency, added:

> "... he did have a violent temper and a terrible mean streak, and it took very little to set him off. In those fits of rage, he was a very dangerous man, and he certainly appeared capable of killing. He would be nice one second, and stare off like he was lost, and then – boom! – tremendous force."

The age-old tale of criminals joining the Army to escape prosecution in America undoubtedly lured the young man, who enlisted soon after his mysterious arrival. Dries joined the US Army under the command of a Colonel named Tom Parker.

That would be the identity that he would assume, steal and carefully maintain for the remainder of his life. While in the Army, Parker went AWOL (absent without leave) and paid the price: he spent an extended period in solitary confinement and emerged with a serious mental illness that ended his tour of duty.

Again, Alana Nash writes:

> "By the time Parker was taken from confinement on April 18, his speech was an incoherent rush of sound, punctuated by terrifying bursts of paranoia and rage. The Army doctor had seen this type of psychotic breakdown before and, suspecting schizophrenia, had Private Parker moved to the guarded lockup ward at the base hospital for observation and treatment...On

> August 11, 1933, after two months of treatment, a medical board consisting of three army surgeons decided that Private Parker was ready to rejoin society. However, he would never again be fit for military duty. They prepared his certificate of disability, repeating the diagnosis – "Constitutional Psychopathic State" – that would forever stigmatize him as a mental patient."

At the tender young age of 24, Tom Parker was already a murderer, scam artist, conman, and mental patient aimlessly wandering the American countryside. But he wasn't just any type of mental patient; he was the most dangerous kind – a psychopath. According to a special research project of the Quantum Future School entitled *The Psychopath - The Mask of Sanity*, a psychopath is explained as:

> "Imagine - if you can - not having a conscience, none at all, no feelings of guilt or remorse no matter what you do, no limiting sense of concern for the well-being of strangers, friends, or even family members. Imagine no struggles with shame, not a single one in your whole life, no matter what kind of selfish, lazy, harmful, or immoral action you had taken."

This is the Colonel Tom Parker who drove Elvis Presley to the very brink of mental, physical, and financial ruin, and in the end arranged to have him killed. The obvious question in regards to Tom Parker is: why didn't Elvis Presley, with all of his money and influence, check out his manager and break free of this insane man?

There are multiple answers to this question. The quickest answer is that he already had the appearance of legitimacy. By the time Parker had met Elvis he was already well established in the entertainment-management business with a proven track record of successfully managing almost a dozen stars.

Aside from Eddy Arnold's personal warning of Parker being hard to work with, there was no reason for any real suspicion or concern. Digging deeper, even if Elvis was suspicious, there would have been no records to check.

There were no birth certificates, no fingerprints and no lineage to be traced. Prior to his Army record, Tom Parker simply didn't exist in the United States, and those Army records would soon vanish by way of powerful friends who were well paid out of Presley's pocketbook.

Colonel Parker had an uncanny ability of gravitating to the top of every group and making sure that he met the biggest and most important players on his way up the ladder. This was a skill that he honed to perfection as he positioned himself within the power elite of show-business and organized crime.

Parker, who befriended both governmental and Mafia figures, confided in mobster Milton Prell about the delicate nature of his illegal-alien status. Prell, a mild-mannered man with numerous contacts, agreed to help clean up the fragmented military and other records that could lead to the discovery and exposure of Andreas van Kuijk.

The price? A piece of the action. This extortion money would rear its head in the form of Presley's new contract, which increased the Colonel's take from 25-75 to a full 50-50 split, with the additional 25% going directly to the mob and its spider web of power-brokers.

In fact, at the same time Colonel Parker negotiated with RCA to buy back all of Elvis' record royalties, which put as much money in Parker's pocket as Presley's, a mysterious fire destroyed Tom Parker's Army files that were housed in the National Personnel Records Center in St. Louis, Missouri. Parker's desperation to bury his illegal-alien background escalated as the years went by, and peaked with the RCA royalties deal.

In 1980 the Presley family hired attorney Blanchard E. Tual to handle affairs of Elvis Presley's estate. In response to the many questions regarding the sale of the royalties back to RCA he stated the following;

> *"In 1973, Elvis was only thirty-seven years old, and it was illogical for him to consider selling a lifetime worth of annuity from his catalogue of over 700 songs. The tax implications alone should have prohibited such an agreement, or at least prohibited it without further tax investigation... thus I must state that Colonel Parker and RCA (Elvis' recording company) were probably guilty of collusion, conspiracy, fraud, misrepresentation, bad faith and overreaching."*

The motivation for making the RCA royalty deal wasn't to help Elvis out of his financial jam, as Parker professed. The Colonel's real motivation was to raise the bounty necessary for Prell. Shortly after the deal was struck and the money changed hands, Prell arranged to have all traces of Parkers military records destroyed by fire.

Within days of the arrangement the National Personnel Records Center in St. Louis, Missouri were reduced to ashes and along with them all traces of Colonel Tom Parker's dirty little secret. Presley was clueless, but in reality, Parker didn't work for Presley – Parker worked for the mob, and for any side deal he could throw together with the name Elvis Presley on it.

Elvis was the money maker, Parker was the deal maker and the mob squeezed as much cash out of the two as possible. By mid-August of 1977, the only thing that stood in the way of the mob getting the flood of money that would be funneled through Boxcar Enterprises and into Colonel Parker's hands was Elvis Presley himself.

When Parker couldn't work Elvis to death, as he'd tried to do in the 2 years prior, he wasn't about to sit around and go broke at the gambling tables waiting for Elvis to die. Elvis was starting to get himself in better physical condition, and every time he was admitted to the hospital with a physical ailment he rebounded a stronger and more lucid man.

Little-by-little, Elvis was getting his life back in order, and the people around him were catching onto Colonel Parker's scheme. Perhaps the first person to realize what Parker was trying to do was one of Presley's oldest friends, Lamar Fike. Nash, in *The Colonel,* quoted Fike as he explains how he told Parker over and over again that he was killing Elvis, and that Elvis was a very sick man.

Parker responded by saying *"Just as long as we keep doing the dates, we don't have to worry."* Also as quoted by Nash is Byron Raphael who claimed that Parker knew Elvis was being worked to death and that a living Elvis *"had become an impediment to his (Parker's) management style and ambition".*

In early 1977, Elvis and a group of his friends were in Hawaii on vacation and Elvis was looking and feeling better that he had in years. On that vacation he discussed losing weight and getting into better shape. This was music to everyone's ears. He also startled everyone when he publicly revealed his plans to remove Tom Parker as his manager and replace him with Tom Hulett of Concerts West. Hulett, who'd already raised the bar for the new phenomenon of rock tours by handling groups like Led Zeppelin, drooled at the very mention of handling Elvis.

Any manager would have jumped at the chance of handling Elvis as his road show was so successful that it financially towered over industry giants like the Rolling Stones. With Vernon now in charge of Elvis' books, finances, and accounting, it became much easier for him to change his ways.

Larry Geller, Presley's hairdresser, friend and spiritual guide, was one of the few people that Elvis truly listened to, and by the time of the Hawaii vacation in March 1977, Geller had been riding Elvis about getting in better shape and helping him with his diet.

This was the true reason Colonel Parker always had a certain level of disdain for Geller: Geller was working in the opposite direction of Parker's wishes. Geller, along with Fike and few others cared more about Elvis than his bankroll. There weren't many of those people, but they did exist.

Colonel Parker wanted to work Elvis to death so he could get the big *after-death* pay off and Geller wanted very much to keep his friend alive. For this, and a million other reasons, Parker was always paranoid of anyone getting so close to Elvis that could influence him, lead him astray or otherwise undermine the ironfisted control exhibited by the person artificially named Colonel Parker.

Parker simply hated everyone whose opinion, religion or profession could lead Elvis in any direction other than the one he had planned, and Larry Geller was on the top of this list.

During the filming of *Roustabout*, Parker threw Geller and his religious books out of Presley's life, forever forbidding contact between the two men in the same way he had severed contact with Steve Binder. While Parker merely kept conversation between Elvis and Binder stifled, Larry Geller wasn't as lucky.

The interview Geller gave to CMT.com reveals the dark side of Parker – his level of control and the command that his phone calls had with underworld figures. In *The Colonel* Geller tells a horrible story where Parker invited the Geller family to his house for a swim, and later, for ice cream.

They returned home to find all of Larry's files and recordings on spiritualism, church, and astrology had been taken, and the house was ransacked. The intruders took nothing else of value, just the very thing that Colonel Parker wanted away from Geller's contact with Elvis.

Larry piled his terrified family back into his car and went to see Elvis. Elvis downplayed the situation but he also said he knew who the culprits were. This was a startling confession by Presley, almost as if this type of tactic were commonplace.

With the pipeline of Colonel Parker's spies in place all around Presley 24-hours-a-day, even on vacation, word quickly reached Tom Parker about what was openly discussed between Geller and Presley, and how Presley's diet, life habits, and the manager switch would be handled.

To compound his manager problems, no one could have possibly imagined that Elvis and his father would become part of an FBI sting operation against the mob – the JetStar scam.

Unbeknownst to the Presleys, their ill-fated sale of the JetStar to Frederick Pro wasn't the beginning of a scam – it was the end of a series of scams the FBI had been tracking for better than a decade.

The investigation was named Operation Fountain Pen, and the Presleys were now called upon to stand as witnesses against the mob. John Parker in *Elvis: Murdered by the Mob* writes:

> *"The news was flashed to FBI offices in Memphis, and elsewhere, and was received with a mixture of shock, disbelief and even suspicion. A serving FBI agent working on the Presley case, and the associated Operation Fountain Pen at the time, said in 1992 that it was not unnatural that the first thought to cross the minds of those investigating officers involved in the case was foul play."*

The two situations – replacing Colonel Parker and his mafia connections with a new manager, and serving as witness against the mob in Operation Fountain Pen – were connected. With the news from the Hawaii vacation still ringing in their ears, a meeting was called between Parker and his business contacts both in and out of the mob. At the meeting the parties established a few obvious points.

First: Presley had to be murdered.

Second: It had to be done in August of 1977.

Third: It had to look like an accident.

Fourth: All evidence would have to be removed.

Fifth: Everything, from the media, to the autopsy, had to be controlled.

Sixth: They needed to immediately lay the groundwork with the merchandisers and record-pressers to prepare for the huge spike in sales immediately after Elvis' death.

Of all the points discussed at the meeting the most time and painstaking effort was spent discussing the third point, the murder absolutely had to look like an accident. If they failed at that the entire arrangement was at risk.

Murder is a big expense to the mob, and the old days of getting rid of the body or murdering more and more people to extend the cover-up were long gone. No one did it that way anymore, because it involved too many loose ends. With an accident, there's nothing to explain away, no body to dump or bury in concrete, and no one to keep silent.

By the mid-1970s the mob had evolved beyond such clumsy practices, as too many mob bosses in the past went to jail doing things the old way. One of the reasons that the mob and the FBI leaked information between each other was simple.

They were both using the same assassins. After all, the US government has invested a ton of money and training in its people to make sure that their hit men knew how to kill their target and escape undetected. The mob wanted the exact same thing.

This is not so say that all of the FBI or the US government's snipers or members of the Special Forces are murderers for hire. Naturally they aren't, but we have to come to the realization that there are bad people in this world, and regardless of the prestige and the level of professionalism that exists within those organizations, bad apples do slip through.

The reality is that certain individuals are guns for hire and that their phone numbers are easily found on the speed dial of some very important people when the opportunity arises. These people may be retired, or on active duty, but they are professionals in their craft.

Professional assassins take weeks or even months to analyze a target. They examine their bad habits, likes and dislikes, their friends, and even their schedule to design a mode of murder that is especially designed for them.

If a target liked to do drugs, they'd make sure there is a "hot dose" to create an overdose, so when the cause of death was revealed, it would be easily swallowed, and no one would ask questions. In that instance, media coverage to explain the murder away would be easily accepted by the public with little work.

It happens every day on the evening news. *"So and so died today of an overdose. He / she was a known drug user for many years. Sports and weather next. . ."*

It happens so frequently that it's almost expected, and no one ever sees a red flag. If a target likes fast cars, there'd be a brake failure. If a target went jogging, someone would run him over and then flee the scene, and so on.

It wouldn't be long before a professional assassin, could narrow down the method, mode, time, and route to *"make it look like an accident,"* and there were plenty of people who wanted Elvis Presley dead.

Once all of the RCA record-stamping plants, photos, posters and other gift-shop merchandising were set for production with all of the proper licensing agreements in place, only one thing was necessary before the mafia could recoup its gambling losses from Parker, and Parker could reap his gigantic rewards: Presley needed to be eliminated.

This was easy to do. Imagine how much danger the FBI had created for Presley as they put him behind the thinnest veil of secrecy. Here was a man who couldn't quietly go anywhere because of the media's wanting eye, yet the FBI knew he was staying in mafia-run hotel-casinos for months at a time, hiding FBI agents who were investigating the mob and posing them as band members?

Certainly the FBI knew that in the mid-1970s the mob had bugged every Las Vegas hotel room as they were always on the lookout for spies and leaks that were out to penetrate their rackets. Beyond any doubt the FBI had to know Elvis would eventually be exposed.

Decades later, the intensity of this mob activity was well covered in the movie *Casino*, where actor Joe Pesci played Nicky Santoro. Santoro was based on a real-life mob enforcer named Anthony "Tony the Ant" Spilotro, who was sent to Las Vegas to protect mob gaming operations.

In the movie, actor Robert De Niro stars as Sam "Ace" Rothstein – a top gambling handicapper who's called by the mob to oversee their casino operations. Robert De Niro's character was based on Frank "Lefty" Rosenthal, who ran the Stardust, Fremont and Hacienda for a string of very powerful mob families.

In Las Vegas, Spilotro was reunited with his boyhood friend Rosenthal and worked together to skim casino profits from the Midwestern mafia families in Chicago, Kansas City, St. Louis and Milwaukee. Spilotro was a ruthless mob enforcer and the FBI was seriously outmatched.

According to the organized crime encyclopedia:

"There was a 70% increase in murders in Las Vegas following Spilotro's arrival." "When Spilotro gained control of Las Vegas, he is alleged to have murdered Frank "the Bomp"

Bompensiero. Bompensiero was the consigliere (family advisor) of the "Mickey Mouse Mafia" (La Cosa Nostra family in California), but may have been cooperating with the FBI and was viewed as an embarrassment to the bosses in the Midwest. Spilotro was indicted in Chicago for the murder of Leo Foreman, a real estate agent/loan shark, who had made the mistake of throwing Sam DeStefano out of his office, in May 1963. Foreman was eventually lured to Sam's home to play cards. There, Foreman was tortured by repeatedly being stabbed with an ice pick and had pieces of his flesh cut out, before being shot and killed."

"According to former Willow Springs, Illinois police chief Michael Corbitt, rumors on the street implicated Spilotro in the murder of former Chicago Outfit boss Sam Giancana. The FBI believes Spilotro was also involved in the murder of loan shark enforcer William "Action" Jackson, who worked for Sam DeStefano in the 1950s and 1960s. The Chicago Outfit thought Jackson had become an FBI informant in 1961. Spilotro allegedly took Jackson to a meat packing plant, where he hung him by a meat hook inside the rectum and then crippled Jackson by smashing his knees with a hammer and poking his genitals with an electric cattle prod. Jackson was left near death for three days before finally succumbing to his injuries."

However fictitious the movie *Casino* was, the Mob – vs - FBI wresting match in Las Vegas during those years was very real, and far worse than the movie portrayed. Knowing this, one must ask why the FBI would put Elvis Presley in the middle of a situation that they knew would result in Elvis being exposed?

The only logical answer is that they were eager to have him eliminated. It was obvious for any number of reasons that the FBI used Elvis as bait to catch very bad men. John Parker in *Elvis: Murdered by the Mob* writes:

> *"The FBI, it was well known, leaked like a sieve. It was believed that leaders of organized crime could get to know the contents of any FBI report within twenty-four hours of it being filed in the system, if not sooner."*

It's obvious that the FBI and the mob were both in on the murder of Elvis Presley and that's why it's been covered up and suppressed with such success at every level of government. Everything from the medical examiner's ridiculous cause of death (a stopped heart) to the mysterious theft of Dan Warlick's notes from his car on the night of the Graceland's investigation were not random events.

They were planned to cover up the murder evidence, and to ensure that the truth would never be told. It's long past time that everyone is made aware of the truth: Elvis Presley insisted on poking his nose in very dangerous places where it simply didn't belong, he pissed off the wrong people, and it cost him his life.

Throughout this book I have repeatedly mentioned that Elvis provided cover for FBI agents, now the time has come to reveal how this information came into being. On the wall in Graceland's trophy room hangs a framed letter from the US Government thanking Elvis for his involvement in a high-profile investigation.

In 1990, researcher Maria Columbus contacted the United States government and made an official inquiry into the existence of the letter. She wanted to know why Elvis had received such an honor. The response from the government was carefully worded, guarded and vague, but it did confirm that from 1975 through 1976 Elvis had provided cover in his band for some of the FBI's best agents to go undercover and investigate the Las Vegas mob.

When Columbus went public with what she had learned, the world dropped its jaw. Not being satisfied with their simplistic answer she began to expand her probe and make further inquiries. After two additional letters and three phone calls the governmental responses to her requests abruptly ended. Columbus had hit the same brick wall that I hit, and that Geraldo Rivera hit at every level in 1979.

I needed more information than Columbus had, but had no idea how to go about getting it. In the fifth year of my research, after I thought the trail was completely cold, I got lucky. I stumbled upon someone (who I cannot name) who me put in touch with one of the agents.

It took a great effort to find and contact her, but my struggle for truth didn't end there. After I asked to speak with her regarding the 33-year-old case, she avoided me like I was the grim reaper. For almost a year I left phone messages about once a month explaining my intention but each message ended without a whisper of a reply. Finally I left an envelope with her doorman.

The note inside did the trick. I told her that I wouldn't print her name and that I would let her read and approve the manuscript before it went to press. With that, two things happened. She agreed to talk with me, and I gave her the fictions moniker of Grace to hide her identity.

Grace was well aware of Elvis' involvement and cooperation within the FBI. She was also well aware that his life was in grave danger. During our interview she shared with me the names of the three agents, two were male and one was female, and told me that their identities were the main reason why Presley's FBI file remains so heavily redacted.

The redaction wasn't done to protect the agents from the public, it was done to protect the agents, and their families, from being murdered by the same people that murdered Elvis. The target of their involved and elaborate investigation was Frederick Pro. The FBI wanted to know who he was connected to in the Las Vegas mob, and how they were working together.

They were able to obtain their information, but it cost one of the undercover agents his life. Unbeknownst to anyone outside of the two groups, Elvis Presley was in the middle of a swarm of Mafia and FBI activity and the murder timeline for everyone involved – from Milton Prell, to Frederick Pro, Colonel Tom Parker and whoever ran the other miscellaneous facets of Parker's merchandising – was the same.

Ironically, that was the same timeframe that the FBI needed Elvis and Vernon to stand trial against the mob in their sting operation, and both mechanisms had been set in motion. By late July the FBI had finished their probe and had enough evidence to convict the worldwide Mafia ring that had defrauded countless people of untold millions on multiple charges.

On August 15th, the FBI prepared arrest warrants for seven men in various cities around the world in connection with the Operation Fountain Pen scam. All of the men were located and were ready to be apprehended the following day, when the unthinkable suddenly happened.

On August 16th, 1977, every television set around the world flashed the incredible news that Elvis Presley, the FBI's key witness, was mysteriously found dead. You would be the biggest fool in the world if you thought this was a mere coincidence.

As I poured over the 663 pages in Presley's FBI files and investigated the numerous interviews and facts that were gathered, it became very obvious to me that Grace was telling the truth.

But what Grace failed to mention, and what I discovered long afterward, was that Elvis Presley had more than one FBI file. While it was true that he had an FBI file under his own name, he also had FBI files under his many aliases as well.

In each file the amount of redaction was incredible, as the bureau continued to protect the identities of the agents. Within those files I quickly learned that throughout the 1970s Elvis was a victim of many assassination and extortion attempts. These facts go far beyond my singular opinion.

Monty Nicholson, a Los Angeles County Sheriff's investigator and author of *The Presley Arrangement* states the following:

> "Recently Gail Giorgio (Elvis author and researcher) and myself viewed FBI documents obtained by Gail. In these documents Elvis was the subject of numerous death threats. Some of these threats came from well-known underground figures and it was also common knowledge that an undercover agent traveled as one of Elvis' band members." Gail Brewer-Giorgio added the following: "I've read 663 FBI files on Elvis Presley, and his life was in danger – it's clear by the FBI reports. There were serious assassination threats against him."

The very first edition of this book was in 2013. Back then I was unaware that Elvis had more than one FBI file. During my interview with Grace I learned that he also had other FBI files under his FBI code names and aliases. Those too were highly redacted. This begs several questions: what is the US government hiding, and why are they continuing to hide it?

Are co-conspirators involved in Presley's murder still in power somewhere within the US government or the Mafia? It's beyond tolerance that FBI files that have been released to the public under the Freedom of Information Act (F.O.I.A.) should continue to black out names after several decades. What do they have to hide?

In a related matter, I myself ran headfirst into a brick wall with a member of the US government when trying to investigate and establish my facts to write this book. For many months I puzzled over the condition of Presley's body when it was discovered.

After all, if indeed the body was as contorted, black and vulgar in appearance as many claim, how could he have had an open-casket service? The more I dug into it, the less sense it made.

Since the medical examiner was obviously distorting facts, and the so-called "witnesses" at the scene cannot seem to decide where the body was found, the position of the body, or the degree of liver mortis, and Dan Warlick's notes were stolen, the only path to truth on the subject would be to interview the EMTs.

I surmised that since the EMTs were only doing their daily duties and have no ulterior motives to withhold information, they'd be worth speaking with. I first began searching for previous interviews from either of the two paramedics – Charles Crosby or Ulysses Jones.

I discovered a 1979 interview between Geraldo Rivera and Ulysses Jones, but the contents of the interview focused on the possibility of a drug death, and did not contain the information that I was seeking.

I was unable to locate Charles Crosby to solicit a comment, but in 2008 I located Ulysses Jones, who was part of the Tennessee government serving in the House of Representatives.

After leaving numerous messages for Mr. Jones over the course of three months at both his Memphis and Nashville offices requesting a very brief interview either by phone or at his office, I received no reply to my requests.

I was puzzled as to why a man who gave so many interviews over the years and was even interviewed by Albert Goldman for his 1981 book *Elvis* would suddenly avoid the subject entirely.

The answer came in the dates the interviews happened. Ulysses Jones was elected to the Legislature in 1986, and after joining the ranks of the same government that shunned the truth, he would afford no more clarity on the matter.

I couldn't blame Jones, who by all accounts was a very good politician until his death on November 9th 2010, but the stark reality of the governmental brick wall is alive and well in the cover up of the truth in the State of Tennessee.

In 1979 Geraldo Rivera voiced similar frustration regarding the indifference of the local government while he was filming his ABC network special for 20/20. He hit the same brick wall. His on-camera comments are as follows:

> *"The official investigation into the death must rank among the worst and most unprofessional investigations of this type ever made. For whatever reason or motive, essentially no real effort was ever made to truly unearth the circumstances of Elvis Presley's death. It seems almost as if the city of Memphis itself does not care to know the truth about the death of its most prominent citizen."*

It became clear that when one looked at the surface issue of Presley's death, and then followed the rabbit hole to the bottom, the logical end was the US government.

Why? Presley's misuse of his federal Narcotics badge, as well as all of the other police agency badges that he obtained for himself and members of his entourage, became a nuisance and many complaints were recorded.

One such incident involved a man whom Elvis suspected of stealing one of his favorite diamond rings. The man boarded an airplane to fly out of Las Vegas for the East Coast. While the plane was taxiing the runway, Elvis chased the plane down flashing his Federal Narcotics Badge and ordered the plane to stop.

The pilot did as he was ordered. Elvis boarded the plane, found the man and roughed him up in his seat. Could you imagine this scene?! The incident took 45 minutes, which upset all of the airline's scheduled flights throughout the balance of the day, to say nothing of the man nearly filing suit against the airline.

Such misuse of federal credentials was a constant embarrassment to the Bureau, and complaints about Elvis' behavior became more and more numerous. Elvis didn't seem to understand that he was jeopardizing the safety of the agents who were touring with his band, who were supposed to be under tight cover.

Through these and other actions, Elvis Presley was stirring up both the mafia in Las Vegas and the federal government in such a fashion that something needed to be done and both sides were in agreement. For the federal government, the decision was an easy one to make.

They simply baited the hook with something they never wanted in the first place and in turn caught the shark they were after. The murder of Elvis Presley removed one of the federal government's major headaches, led to the arrest of Frederick Pro and everyone else in Operation Fountain Pen to end a decade-long FBI sting operation, generated multiple millions of dollars in profits for Parker and Prell through Boxcar Enterprises, and ensured that Parker's $30 million gambling marker would be paid in full.

All sides of these leaky organizations were in total agreement, and now even the agents traveling in Elvis' band began to gather information against Elvis as well. Colonel Parker also supplied a wealth of information.

Unknowingly, Joe Esposito would relay every tiny detail to Parker, being the dutiful employee that he was, Parker would relay everything to the mob, and the mob would relay the info back to the FBI. With that, the circle of information necessary to murder Presley was complete.

The opposite was also happening: the Mob was gathering information about Elvis' activities in Las Vegas through their sources and wiretaps, circulating the info back through Milton Prell, "Moe" Dalitz and then to Colonel Parker. By the time August 1977 appeared on the calendar, the two organizations knew more about Elvis than Elvis did.

They knew the lackadaisical habits of his valet, they knew that three of his most highly trained bodyguards had been recently fired, leaving a huge gap in his security team, and they had the blueprints of Graceland (which had recently been renovated).

They knew all of Graceland's entrances and exits, knew exactly when and who would be flying out of town to start the next leg of the tour and their habits and schedules, they knew their mode of travel, and they knew when Graceland would be most vacant and most accessible.

They knew the time of day that Elvis was most vulnerable for a one-on-one encounter with an assassin, and most importantly they knew that Presley's upstairs suite was padded with thick-tufted Naugahyde, and that when it was remodeled Elvis added special soundproofing so that he could sleep during the day and the downstairs activities would not disturb him.

They also knew that anything that happened upstairs could not be heard anywhere in the house, even if someone screamed for help. From this information they devised a plan for exactly when and where the murder would happen. It would have to happen on the eve of a new tour while almost everyone was missing from Graceland and already on location.

And most importantly, the murder would have to occur in either Elvis' bedroom or his bathroom study, as the sound-deadening building material was heaviest in those rooms.

Numerous agents and double agents on both sides of both organizations – the mob and the FBI – had been gathering this information to ensure that the 'everybody–wins' murder would happen and never be fully investigated.

The only thing left to plan was the actual mode of entry the assassin would take. All of Graceland's windows had long since had iron-caged bars installed over them, so entry there wasn't an option. So how could one gain unsuspecting entry to a heavily guarded and gated building?

I remember witnessing one such event when attending my local county fair. I stood in line with my friends to buy tickets and get our hands stamped when a pizza delivery boy walked up to the gate in front of us holding a pizza box.

The person at the gate stamped his hand and allowed him to enter to make his delivery. As luck would have it, we walked in just behind him – in time to watch him walk ten feet, throw the empty pizza box in the trash and hop on his favorite ride.

The deed was done, and free access was authorized and established. We all shook our heads in disbelief and laughter, but the free and unsuspecting entry was gained and the deed was done before anyone noticed. Could it have been the same with the Presley murder?

At 9:30am on August 16th 1977, the day Elvis was murdered, a US mail truck was given permission to enter the gates of Graceland to hand deliver a certified letter from Paul Lichter to Elvis. Paul is the founder of the Elvis Presley Unique Record Club and the special delivery letter was for Elvis Presley's eyes only.

In a recent telephone conversation Mr. Lichter explained to me that he had mailed the same letter to Vernon Presley and Colonel Parker. The content of the letter was to refute the lurid allegations that had recently been printed about Elvis in the newly published *Bodyguard Book*.

To the naked eye, the only thing that happened that morning was a US mail truck drove up to the front door of Graceland, the postal worker rang the front door bell, handed the letter to Elvis in exchange for his signature, and the two men parted ways. The driver took some time to properly arrange his paperwork, readied his inventory of future deliveries within the truck, and then drove out of Graceland.

The exchange was very non-descript, routine and innocent, but that's not all that happened. The driver of the truck wasn't just dropping something off – he was picking something up and driving it out. For starters, the postman who was driving the mail truck wasn't the normal mailman whom every one of the Graceland guards was accustomed to seeing.

In fact, he wasn't a mailman at all. In the years that followed, many researchers established the bitter fact that this man wasn't employed by the Memphis Post Office, or any Post Office. To date no one has ever been able to establish his identity, and that's because his job was to do more than deliver the mail.

In 1992, the Presley Commission was formed to launch a serious examination into the death of Elvis Presley in a professional and research-based manner. When the special-delivery receipt was examined, the Commission asked the burning questions.

The following quote can be found at elvisinfonet.com: *"Why was the mail carrier different that day from the usual carrier? The signature on the receipt was not that of the usual carrier. In an interview with a supervisor at the Post Office, the name on the return slip wasn't even recognized as a regular employee. Who was this carrier, and who did he really work for?"*

The answer was obvious. His watch was synchronized with that of another man who had entered Graceland's property from the rear left of the Graceland lot – crossing through the brush and carport and entering through the back stairway door.

Dressed as a Postal employee, the assassin gained entry with a key that had been given to him days prior when he received the blueprints and his additional instructions. Within a matter of seconds, the man had gained access.

Walking through Lisa Marie's bedroom undetected was an easy feat, as she stated in numerous interviews that she was playing in a different part of the house and was finally sent to bed by Elvis himself at 4am. Soon after Elvis went into his bedroom, she ignored Elvis' bedtime demands and continued playing elsewhere.

From 9:00am onward Graceland was no longer the silent, vacant hull of a house that it had been in previous hours. The maids had shown up for work and had begun their ritual of vacuuming on the lower floors. The deafening silence was broken by the low moaning of vacuum cleaners that resonated up the stairs from the ground floor.

It created the perfect noise buffer. If anything could be heard, which was unlikely, the vacuum cleaners ensured that it would be drowned out. The assassin quietly closed the door to Lisa's bedroom upon exiting, and did the same as he entered the far door to Elvis' bathroom.

Closing the doors was necessary to contain any noise that could be heard. It was a precaution worth taking. From there he slipped into the bathroom. In perfect coordination with his counterpart in the mail truck who drew Elvis to the front door, the assassin quietly grabbed a tall, thin aerosol can from the bathroom counter and tucked it in his back pocket.

From the bathroom counter he moved into place and soaked a rag with chloroform. The assassin's positioning was ideal. He could clearly see Elvis as he entered, and the entry happened right on cue.

THE PATH OF THE ASSASSIN

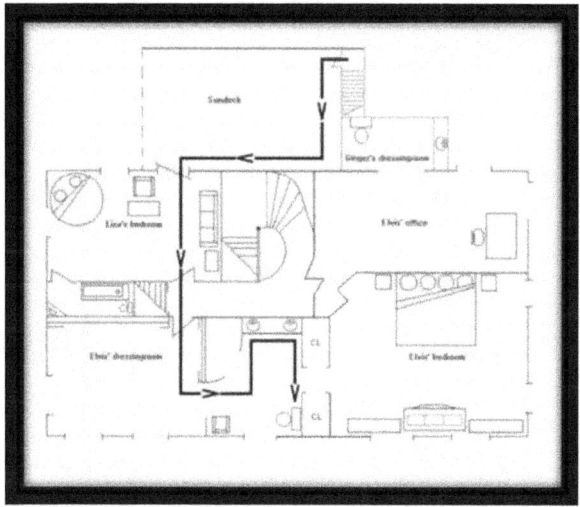

Elvis took the letter, opened it, and tossed it on his office desk. Within moments he walked through the office doorway into his bedroom. Still in a partial drug-induced stupor, Elvis picked up his book and headed for a favorite reading spot – his bathroom.

As Elvis lumbered from his bedroom into the bathroom, his left shoulder passed mere inches from the very man who'd been handsomely paid to murder him. Pictured is the path taken by Elvis as he returned from signing for his special delivery letter.

THE PATH OF ELVIS

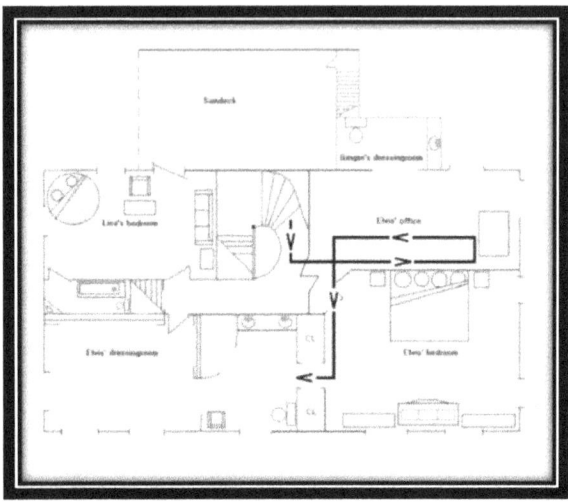

Neither Graceland, which had stood on its 13.8-acre lot since its erection in 1939, nor the far reaches of the globe, would be prepared for what happened next. On this seemingly typical morning, the dwelling would bear the only true witness to America's most controversial death since the public slaughter of President John F. Kennedy 14 years earlier.

The assassin used the heavily chloroformed rag and got behind Elvis, taking him totally off guard. The assassin wrapped Presley's face with the rag and tackled the semi-drugged singer face-first into the carpeting.

With Ginger and Lisa Marie missing, there was no one to hear as Elvis flung the book out of his hand to try and free his face. The book hit the bathroom counter and knocked over some aftershave bottles next to Elvis' sink.

The crash was not heard, nor was the minor scuffle that ensued before Elvis lost consciousness. The impact as Presley's face was jammed into the floor by the force of two men's inertia would smash Presley's nose, creating the pug snout the world would see in the casket days later, and that conspiracy theorists would use to argue the corpse was a wax dummy. Elvis was so drugged that despite his martial-arts training and rooms filled with automatic weaponry he was helpless.

THE MURDER

As Elvis wilted into a limp, unconscious heap on the carpeting – the murderer inflicted a method used by professionals for centuries. This method produces death swiftly and isn't identified through bruises to the corpse. The assassin released the rag soaked with chloroform that he was clutching around Presley's face and reached for the aerosol can that he had in his back pants pocket.

He pressed it in place at the base of Elvis' chin where it met his neck and with the can in place the assassin forced Elvis' head down toward his chest, closing off his oxygen. As the Postal vehicle stalled for time by the front door pretending to adjust the delivery packages, Elvis was losing his battle for life.

In a matter of seconds Presley was lifeless on the floor with bulging eyes, a protruding tongue half bitten off and a deep-blue facial tint. There were no bruises to be found. The suffocation / asphyxiation combined with the chemical used to knock Presley unconscious created the regurgitation of gastric fluids in the shag carpeting that was later cleaned by the maids.

This wet spot on the floor was identified by Dan Warlick during his on scene investigation. In less than 5 minutes, Elvis had been transformed into a motionless lump of dead flesh. With Presley dead, the assassin's task was nearly complete.

In a whirlwind of activity, the assassin replaced the aerosol can on the bathroom counter where it was taken from and administered the calling card of a mob hit; he pulled Elvis's pajama bottoms down to his ankles to add insult to injury.

This is a ritual commonly done by the Sicilian mob to disrespect the murdered man. In fact, the Italian citizens who had suffered under rule of their dictator, Bonito Mussolini, during the Second World War did the same thing to him after his death. In that culture it is the ultimate and final insult.

The only task that remained before the murderous postal impostor could escape was to confuse the scene so no real investigation into the cause of death could ever take place. He planted two drug syringes in Elvis' bedroom and office in plain view so anyone would find them immediately upon inspection.

With the death scene properly clouded with planted evidential decoys, the murderer quickly slinked down Graceland's front staircase, through the front door and into the back of the waiting mail truck.

ESCAPE ROUTE

To be caught at this point would be virtually impossible – all a curious onlooker could see would be the unsuspecting sight of two Postal employees adjusting packages. As the assassin slumped down in the rear of the panel truck, the driver shifted into drive and the engine purred down the driveway.

The same postman who drove past the security guard at the front gate on the way to deliver the letter was the same postman who left the grounds minutes later. The precision of the two men was perfect, and in the tiny span of 60 seconds, they would be off Presley's property, forever to disappear into the bustle and obscurity of the morning traffic. The time was 9:40am, and Elvis Presley had just been murdered in his own home.

This horrible murder would lay undiscovered for hours until Ginger Alden returned to make the discovery and call James Kirk at approximately 2:30 in the afternoon. Kirk was the local contact to the National Enquirer and the person Ginger called in an ill-fated attempt to profit from her concocted story.

By now it should seem obvious that the age old tale of Elvis falling off the toilet and crawling to his death is mere fantasy. In reality, Elvis was not on the toilet at all, which explains why neither the EMTs nor investigator Dan Warlick found anything in the toilet to analyze; and when questioned those present claimed that the toilet had not been flushed. Unbelievably, this is the only part of the story they agreed on.

The entire 'toilet story' had been hastily and sloppily concocted after the fact which fully explains why none of the "witness" stories aligned. By the time the damage control stories had been arranged keeping all the stories straight would be virtually impossible.

After all, something had to explain the location of the body and why it was found nude from the waist down. The only story available to connect those dots would have to involve some lurid toilet story which has never made sense to anyone in 1977, and makes even less sense as the decades have passed.

The discovery of Presley's bloated, discolored and half nude corpse was an identical discovery to that of former heavy weight boxing champion Sonny Liston seven years earlier in Las Vegas.

Liston was also having issues with the mob which ended in the discovery of his corpse and death scene that was an identical fashion to Presley's. This was no coincidence. Paul Lichter, who innocently mailed the certified letter to Elvis that morning, unknowingly sealed Presley's fate. Years later he gave an interview to ClassicBands.com to describe the special delivery and said:

> "Ultimately he signed for the letter. Here's the history: After it happened, I was asked not to discuss it by RCA and the Colonel. After those initial interviews in the days after, I never did. What happened was, the green card, the Post Office gets a card, you get a card back when it's certified, registered." "I got the card back. If you've seen pictures of the receipt, the original receipt was stolen, but we were able to get a copy from the Memphis Post Office...In my book Elvis: The Legend Lives On *there's a picture of it there for anybody to see.*"

In my contact with Mr. Lichter, who has granted me permission to display the Special Delivery notice, he described Elvis as *"a big brother and a father figure"*.

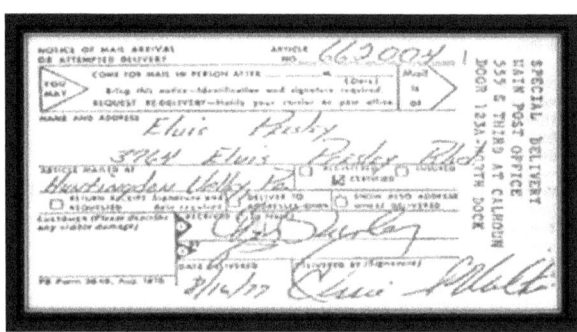

Image Courtesy Of Paul Lichter's Elvis Photo Archives/elvisunique.com

Meanwhile, in the hours after the murder, Colonel Parker knew that it was only a matter of time before Joe Esposito would call with the hysterical news, and with that phone call would begin the second preplanned phase of the murder – the medical cover up.

When the call came Parker was in the presence of Lamar Fike in Portland, Maine and Colonel Parker hardly seemed shaken by the news. In fact, he seemed so unemotional and cold that it made Fike furious. Colonel Parker bellowed to Esposito over the telephone to have the maids completely sanitize the entire contents of the bedroom and the bathroom and in doing so forever hid key evidence necessary to solve the murder.

The rest of the evidence, what little there was, magically disappeared in the presence of the police officers who remained at the scene with Vernon Presley. Immediately after Elvis was taken to the ER and the HARVEY team was dispatched in an attempt to revive the Rock-n-Roll idol who'd been dead for many hours, the next piece of the cover-up puzzle fell into place.

All of Presley's stomach contents were intentionally rinsed down the drain. This is something that only a trained employee of Baptist Memorial Hospital could have done, because no one else would have access. This could have only been an inside job and was the beginning of the medical cover up by the hospital.

With the stomach contents conveniently dripping down the drain of the ER, any chance of a thorough autopsy was gone. This would be a half-hearted autopsy that seemed to intentionally ignore all evidence of foul play.

A Manual of Legal Medicine by Justin Herold, on forensic medicine by strangulation, states the following:

"The face is usually livid and swollen, but occasionally when the arrest of the atmospheric air is complete, it becomes entirely black in color. The pupils are dilated and the eyes assume a staring appearance. The tongue protrudes and may appear wounded.

The extremities are livid and the genital organs often turgid. Occasionally there has been noted hemorrhage from the ears, nose, mouth, and throat."

Compare Herold's information on strangulation with the descriptions of Joe Esposito, Ginger Alden and Ulysses Jones who were the three eyewitnesses to the condition of the corpse.

Joe Esposito:

". . . he noticed that his tongue was out and that he had bitten it. He was unable to push the tongue back into the singer's mouth. In addition to Presley's general stiffness, Esposito said he noticed the cold blue complexion of Elvis's face and neck." – The Death of Elvis

Ulysses Jones:

"When he first entered the bathroom, (Ulysses) Jones said the blue coloration fooled him into thinking the prostrate form was that of a black man, about six feet tall and weighing over 250 pounds. Jones was shocked to learn this was Elvis Presley." – The Death of Elvis

The now-famous Domestic Violence Handbook for Police in Alberta Canada states the following on strangulation:

"Only eleven pounds of pressure placed on both carotid arteries for ten seconds is necessary to cause unconsciousness. However, if pressure is released immediately, consciousness will be regained within ten seconds. To completely close off the trachea, three times as much pressure (33 pounds) is required. Brain death will occur in 4 to 5 minutes, if strangulation persists. Because of unforeseen consequences of injuries from a strangulation attempt that may appear minor to the untrained, police officers at the scene should radio for medics for a medical evaluation of all victims who report being strangled."

According to *Death by Strangulation*, written by Dr. Dean Hawley – an expert on domestic-violence strangulation at the Indiana University School of Medicine – the vast majority of strangulation victims have no visible injuries. Worthy of note is that the group of doctors and specialists assembled at the Presley autopsy were highly skilled in many areas, but not in strangulation. Acting on the information of Dan Warlick, who witnessed two syringes at the death scene, they were far more focused on drugs as the potential cause of death. In their attempts to autopsy the body and remove the organs they actually destroyed the strangulation evidence.

Dr. Hawley writes:

"Medical resuscitation, and organ procurement procedures, work against the pathologist's ability to detect fatal homicidal neck injury. In some

communities, organ procurement procedures are routinely performed, regardless of the circumstances of death. A dissection for heart donation can totally obliterate all evidence of injury by manual strangulation."

Further, in *Death by Strangulation*, Dr. Hawley writes the summation of his thesis on strangulation and explains the first of four mechanisms that strangulation can produce: *"Immediate death from hanging or strangulation can progress from one of four mechanisms: The very first cause is cardiac arrhythmia."*

Again, this was the exact cause of death Dr. Jerry T. Francisco emphatically repeated in 1977. Dr. Hawley explains:

"1. Cardiac arrhythmia may be provoked by pressure on the carotid artery nerve ganglion (carotid body reflex) causing cardiac arrest."

What Dr. Francisco conveniently left out was *"why"*. What caused Elvis Presley's cardiac arrhythmia? According to every doctor at the autopsy, Elvis Presley had no cardiac diseases, and at age 42, he was years away from having any serious heart trouble.

Dr. Hawley continues:

"Further, if even a small force is applied in just the right anatomic area, the force may obviate the normal anatomic protections of the neck musculature and skeleton. A small woman can

easily strangle a large man. The U.S. Army trains 'close range combatives' to use strangulation as a mechanism of lethal force."

Since the FBI and the mob have leaked information between each other for ages, the "right anatomic area" has been well researched and located by both the US government's special agents, freelance professional assassins and mob hit men. It's well within the best interest of both of the organizations to study, learn and have adept knowledge in these areas.

The written works of Gael B. Strack, JD and Dr. George McClane, titled *How to Improve Your Investigation and Prosecution of Strangulation Cases*, sheds possibly the most light on the potential that Elvis was strangled by claiming:

> *"Focusing on the visible signs of strangulation, most victims lacked physical evidence of being strangled. They either had no visible injury (50%) or their injuries were too minor to photograph (35%). Today, we know that strangulation is one of the most lethal forms of domestic violence: Unconsciousness may occur within seconds and death within minutes. Victims may have no visible injuries whatsoever."*

If the first clue that Elvis Presley was strangled – or rather, had his windpipe manually closed off by an attacker using a form of lethal training was the onset of cardiac arrhythmia. The second clue comes in the form of the very definition of strangulation itself.

Strack and McClane define strangulation as; *"a form of asphyxia (lack of oxygen) characterized by closure of the blood vessels and/or air passages of the neck as a result of external pressure on the neck."*

This all sounds simple and feasible enough when you consider the position that Presley was found in. Already covered in Dr. Hawley's work were the bulging eyes, protruding tongue, and blue-black color of the face and neck. Strack and McClane further explain the lethal effects of strangulation.

"The victim will lose consciousness by any one or all of the following: Blocking of the carotid arteries (depriving the brain of oxygen), blocking of the jugular veins (preventing deoxygenated blood from exiting the brain), and closing off the airway, causing the victim to be unable to breathe."

These are Joe Esposito's comments about when he rolled Elvis over. Thompson and Cole's *The Death of Elvis* noted:

"Beside the stretcher Esposito told Nichopoulos that he heard Elvis breathe in the bathroom when he turned him over and felt him expel some air from his lungs."

Obviously, Elvis had air trapped in his lungs that was interrupted and trapped when he slumped and his windpipe was closed off.

The excess oxygen couldn't escape in the position he was found in, but when he was rolled over the residual air escaped, giving Esposito both a false sense of hope and a mystery worthy of discussing with the doctor.

Dr. Nick, knowing that just about anything can happen at death, passed this information off and misunderstood its importance. The final clues to the strangulation of Elvis Presley came in the reading of a textbook titled *Medical Jurisprudence and Toxicology* written by John J. Reese MD.

Dr. Reese is a professor of Medical Jurisprudence and Toxicology at the University of Pennsylvania, vice president of The Medical Jurisprudence Society of Philadelphia, Physician to St. Joseph's Hospital, member of the College of Physicians of Philadelphia and corresponding member of the New York Medico Legal Society.

Needless to say his qualifications and the book itself were the holy grail of information for strangulation evidence. Dr. Reese notes:

> *"Death results, in most cases, from the combined effect of the deprivation of atmospheric air producing apnoea, from congestion of the brain, due to the pressure upon the jugulars, preventing the return of blood*

from the brain. The appearance of one strangled are usually very distinctly marked: These are livid and swollen face; staring eyes, with dilated pupils and protruding tongue, which may have been bitten; livid extremities; flattened larynx; blood may issue from the nose, mouth, or even ears; the face, neck, chest, and eyes are studded with ecchymoses; the genital organs, frequently turgid..."

The following, from *The Death of Elvis*, is relevant to the strangulation discovery:

"He (Warlick) did note that the body had 'congestion to the face and upper torso" "Next the team began checking the abdominal organs, all of which proved to be large. Warlick said all of Elvis' abdominal organs were oversized." "His spleen weighed 340 grams. A normal spleen might weigh about 75 grams." "Warlick checked Elvis's nose, observed a trickle of blood seeping from the nostrils."

Dr. Reese notes in his medical textbook:

"It should not be forgotten that the marks of homicidal strangulation may often be discovered many weeks, or even years after burial. One is mentioned by Wharthon and Stille' (Med. Juisp. Vol. II, P. 830), where, after thirty-eight days' interment, the evidence of strangulation was obtained chiefly from the striking contrast of the integuments of the neck with those of the rest of the body. There was a white, shriveled space

over the larynx, half an inch broad; also a groove around the neck, of a blackish-brown color and parchment-like appearance; this condensed skin was difficult to cut, and its section was perfectly dry and yellowish."

From everything that has been written and researched about strangulation, the autopsy was done so fast that the true evidence of asphyxia from either windpipe blockage or strangulation was never discovered. With all that we now know versus what we knew in 1977 regarding the stealth of strangulation, and with every doctor at the autopsy looking for drugs instead of a homicide, the corpse was torn apart, thus destroying the evidence forever.

With the rushed and fumbled autopsy now complete, and all the evidence of strangulation either purposely ignored or concealed, the Elvis Presley case was closed and the official cause of death was listed as *"cardiac arrhythmia from undetermined causes."*

In other words, his heart stopped beating and no one has any idea why. Back at Graceland, the only lasting residual effects of the murder were minor signs of a struggle that appeared in Dan Warlick's investigation photos and notes, which were conveniently stolen out of Warlick's car later that night outside of his apartment. The cover-up was complete – all loose ends of the conspiracy were now trimmed.

The murder, the cover up at Graceland, the EMTs, the ER, and even the autopsy were coordinated perfectly. In his interview with ClassicBands.com, Paul

Litcher sums up the events better than anyone ever could when he says:

> "If you want to be a conspiracy guy, how did RCA have all those millions of records ready to ship to every store within an hour? How did the Colonel have all the memorial posters and T-shirts they were selling at the gate before the body was returned to the house?"

Separately, ABC reporter Geraldo Rivera in doing his research for his upcoming 20/20 TV special came to the same conclusion. Rivera spoke the following into the camera and asked viewers to consider the following:

"

- *No real police investigation was ever made. At 9:00 in the evening on the same day Elvis died, before it was medically or scientifically possible to know for sure why or how he died, the Memphis police declared this case closed.*

- *Dan Warlick was the man in charge of the medical examiner's investigation. Dr. Jerry T. Francisco, his boss, claimed Warlick had made an extensive search for drugs at Elvis' home, Graceland. In fact, Warlick admitted to us that he had never searched the trailer where all the drugs were kept.*

- *Elvis's stomach contents were destroyed without ever having been analyzed.*

- *There was no coroner's inquest.*

- *The Shelby County district attorney was never officially notified or asked to determine if there were any violations of criminal law.*

- *All of the photographs of the death scene, all the notes of the medical examiner's investigation, and all of the toxicological reports allegedly prepared by the medical examiner are missing from the official files.*

- *Officials of the county government believe there has been a cover-up.* "

This is either the sloppiest and most hap-hazard investigation known to mankind, which is hard to fathom considering we are talking about the biggest star in the world, or there is an underlying motivation for everyone to ignore their duties and their job titles. No one could be this obtuse. Now that you have fallen down this rabbit hole are you willing to see how deep it really goes?

6
The Requiem

"Vernon would pursue the possibility of foul play himself, in the days ahead, but the possibility of an open inquiry into the death of Elvis Presley was already being blocked."

-The Death of Elvis-

Once all the facts of the Presley cover-up have been fully exposed and analyzed, the gravity of the murder itself isn't all that different from any other murder that the cooperating agencies within our government have patterned for better than half a century.

In the past, any high-profile person who influenced the population contrary to the government's desires, or pesters the "powers that be", would be met with a similar fate. Back in those days, the Mob and the US government were in many cases one and the same. People like J. Edgar Hoover and Lyndon Johnson both had enormous pull and a functional knowledge of the "who's who" to get things done.

Hoover's reluctance to prosecute the mob is well documented and he skated around the issue for many years. These "elimination decisions" are fostered and carried out by people who aren't subject to four-year elections and whose names aren't commonly spoken.

They are at the behest of people who dominate the highest levels of those organizations and whose motives are kept in a distant vault that is far removed from the desires of average hardworking citizens.

The distended roots of such agencies, and their murderous involvement, can be traced as far back in American history as the assassination of President Abraham Lincoln, whose seating arrangements at Ford's theater on the night of April 14th 1865, were leaked by our own government to his assassins.

The modern-day strain of these agencies started largely in the aftermath of World War II. Elvis, like the rest of the naive American public, remained totally unaware that his country was changing from the inside out.

The change started in the early 1950s and intensified as the decades wore on. Looking at Elvis Presley's murder as a singular event apart from the landscape within which it happened is like studying a blade of grass without looking at the whole lawn.

The same year that Elvis Presley skyrocketed to fame, J. Edgar Hoover was transforming the FBI to be an attack force. Hoover was entering his 22nd year as FBI director and was fed up with the lackluster performance of the US Supreme Court and the Justice Department.

Everyone from Communists to high-level criminals that he delivered to the prosecution's doorstep were walking free and laughing in the bureau's face.

Year after frustrating year, Hoover was made out to be a stooge and by the mid-1950's he was fully involved in transforming the FBI from an above-board law enforcement agency to include a secret network of bullies and thugs.

This 'New FBI', as he called it, would get their way by any legal or illegal means necessary. Never again would he be made out to be a joke in the courts, or worse yet, the court of public opinion. The CIA soon followed suit expanding their bag of tricks as well.

If the new arms of the government had existed at an earlier time in the United States, young Presley's bump and grind stage show wouldn't have been accepted. In fact, he may have been eliminated right away.

To soothe the nation's outrage against this polarizing young star, Hoover and his New FBI, would have probably terrorized Presley's family or threatened him into submission.

If that didn't work, then they would have employed physical tactics to get him to bend to their will. Lastly, if none of that worked they would have killed him and made it look like an accident, spinning it to their satisfaction in the media.

Hoover would have done anything necessary to stop the uproar of their civilian inventory and lull them back to sleep, but time was not on the government's side, so Presley had to be drafted into the armed forces to remove him from being the societal nuisance that parents thought he was.

Numerous works reflect the level at which the government went to influence and manipulate their inventory. Mark Zepezauer writes about such projects in his book *The CIA's Greatest Hits*. He notes:

"From 1959 to at least 1974, the CIA used its domestic organizations to spy on thousands of US citizens whose only crime was disagreeing with their government's policies."

During these years the government designed many projects of mass manipulation that started with Hoover's retooled FBI and ended with Operation Chaos.

Operation Chaos was designed to infiltrate, disrupt and destroy dissident groups by any means necessary, and taking a page out of Hoover's book, to win without bringing them to court.

When Nixon was elected President, he was fed up with America's dysfunctional Hippie culture who was not supporting America's war effort in Vietnam. In doing so, he merged America's new counterculture protests with the Communist threat and constructed the view that doing drugs was a Communist plot against our nation.

To expand his agenda, Nixon agreed to expand Hoover's manipulation network even farther. This time it included the Huston Plan. The Huston Plan included government sponsored break-ins, mail openings, wiretapping, no knock searches, covert beatings and even assassinations if necessary.

This once again bloated the power of the New FBI and Hoover was elated with Nixon's cooperation. The Huston Plan and its predecessor, Operation Chaos, were both couched in Hoover's new COINTELPRO network. COINTELPRO was the code name for the nation's counterintelligence program, and Hoover wasted no time in exercising it.

With Hoover's new COINTELPRO network vigorously working in the nation's cities, President Nixon was starting to make traction against his enemies among the nations interior.

Nixon thought he had everything figured out until the Monday before Christmas of 1970. The exact date was December 21st and it was the date that Elvis Presley sauntered into the Oval Office wearing three handguns to have a sit down with the President.

Elvis Presley and Richard Nixon had many things in common: they both hated the counterculture movement, street drugs, and what they had turned America into.

With all of these similarities, Presley had no idea that when he met Nixon, they would both fall prey to Hoover's gluttony of control. Anyone who could potentially harm Hoover or got between him and the mob became a target of his wrath. Numerous US Presidents wanted Hoover fired, but every time they set a meeting to terminate him, Hoover appeared clutching a file folder full of blackmail material that he threatened to leak to the media.

It wasn't long before Hoover and his COINTELPRO network were running wild throughout the nation with no one to stop them, and in 1960, when John Kennedy won the presidential election over Richard Nixon, change came to the White House – change that neither J Edgar Hoover, nor Lyndon Johnson liked.

When JFK appointed his brother, Bobby, to the post of US Attorney General, Bobby became both Hoover's superior and Lyndon Johnson's arch enemy. Hoover and Johnson had many things in common. They had been neighbors and good friends for many years. They were also good friends of a fella whose name you may have heard throughout this book, none other than Colonel Tom Parker, and it wouldn't be long before all three men hated Elvis Presley.

Colonel Parker had met Lyndon Johnson through his connection with Frank Sinatra and Salvatore (Sam) Giancana, and their contacts within the FBI, namely, J. Edgar Hoover. The connection between Colonel Parker and President Johnson grew so strong that in the 1964 presidential campaign, Colonel Parker gave his cowboy logo to Johnson for the length of the campaign.

Alanna Nash in *The Colonel* writes:

"Parker zeroed in on one in particular - Texas Senator Lyndon Baines Johnson - and in the fall of '59 volunteered EddyArnold's services when LBJ honored the president of Mexico, Adolfo Lopez Mateos, at his Johnson City Ranch...Two months after the Virginia barbeque, Johnson wrote to Parker using the words that must have seemed golden: 'I hope our paths cross again in the days ahead, and that you always feel free to call on me as your friend at any time for anything.' Apparently, the Colonel did just that. A mere two weeks later, Johnson told him he was certainly 'counting on you to give the office a ring when you get to Washington.'"

Once Johnson bought the house across the street from Hoover, LBJ could do no wrong in Washington. Soon after, every politician Johnson ran against died mysteriously or lost in a rigged election.

In 1937, a congressman died suddenly and Johnson was elected.

In 1941, Senator Sheppard died suddenly and Johnson was elected to fulfill the term.

In 1948, Johnson stole an election from Coke Stevenson. It was later discovered that the 200 votes were alphabetically "stuffed" by "voters" who were dead. Not surprisingly, the FBI refused to investigate.

In 1953–55, throughout the 83rd Congress, nine senators died mysteriously, giving Johnson his desired title of senate majority leader – a post he held until his run for the White House in 1960.

In 1963, Johnson became president when JFK was assassinated, and he made Hoover FBI director for life, an appointment that certainly looked like the perfect Presidential payback.

Like the rest of America, Elvis himself had an obsession with the Kennedy assassination and would watch the Zapruder Film with his friends for endless hours. Elvis believed that President Kennedy, along with his brother, Robert Kennedy, had both been murdered in a governmental conspiracy.

Amazingly, Elvis was in the process of launching his own private investigation into the JFK assassination when he was murdered. In August of 1977, the month Elvis died, the House Select Committee on Assassinations was re-investigating the assassinations of President John F. Kennedy and Dr. Martin Luther King.

The committee and its investigative powers were formed by the solicitation of my friend, Mark Lane. Lane, who is mentioned throughout this book, was a friend of JFK and demanded that the United States Government reinvestigate the Warren Commissions findings.

The committee was formed in 1976 to answer the public's outcry after the Zapruder film was finally shown to the American public on TV in 1975. In the twelve years prior, the US government had withheld this evidence from the American public at the request of FBI director, J. Edgar Hoover.

What the House of Representatives Select Committee had uncovered was so in-depth that some people had to be hushed up, and William Sullivan was one of those people.

Sullivan, J. Edgar Hoover's second in command, was shot and killed by a high-powered rifle while hunting in New Hampshire. Sullivan had just completed a preliminary meeting with investigators of the Committee, but that was only part of the reason for his murder.

Numerous reports were pouring into the FBI that William Sullivan had met with Elvis Presley in an attempt to use Sullivan's inside information of the JFK assassination, combined with Presley's bankroll, to conduct a private investigation for public release.

Such an investigation outraged Colonel Parker, to say nothing of his contacts in the Mob and the FBI. How very odd that by the time the House Select Committee on the Assassinations had completed its investigations, both William Sullivan and Elvis Presley were dead of very suspect and questionable circumstances. Questionable circumstances that looked awfully familiar.

Elvis Presley, along with numerous other politicians and celebrities were eliminated by the government, from within the government, with all evidence removed and no one left accountable. Hoover's vison of controlling the masses was engineered and handcrafted to perfection as the process was used dozens of times.

From the following list it's impossible to believe that every death was accidental, and once you accept that, the next question is how many were really murdered? While looking at the following list remember to bear in mind the legal definition of Conspiracy. If only two of these people were murdered you have a conspiracy on your hands.

YEAR	NAME	CAUSE OF DEATH
1959	Ritchie Valens	Plane crash
1959	Buddy Holly	Plane crash
1959	The Big Bopper	Plane crash
1960	Jesse Belvin	Car accident
1960	Eddie Cochran	Car accident
1962	Marilyn Monroe	Drug overdose
1962	Stuart Sutcliffe	Aneurysm
1963	Sam Cooke	Shooting
1964	Bobby Fuller	Suicide
1966	Ronnie Caldwell	Plane crash
1967	Otis Redding	Plane crash
1967	Jackie Wilson	Heart attack
1967	Brian Epstein	Drug overdose

1968	Frankie Lymon	Drug overdose
1969	Brian Jones	Drowning
1970	Alan Wilson	Drug overdose
1970	Tammi Terrell	Illness
1970	James Ramey	Drug overdose
1970	Mary Ann Ganser	Illness
1970	Jimi Hendrix	Drug overdose
1970	Janis Joplin	Drug overdose
1971	Gene Vincent	Illness
1971	Jim Morrison	Heart attack
1971	Edie Sedgwick	Drug overdose
1971	*Duane Allman	Motorcycle accident
1972	*Berry Oakley	Motorcycle accident
	(* Died 3 blocks from Duane Allman in a similar accident.)	
1972	Les Harvey	Electrocution
1972	Andrea Feldman	Suicide
1973	Gram Parsons	Drug overdose
1973	Bruce Lee	Swollen brain
1973	Jim Croce	Plane crash
1973	Ron McKernan	Illness
1973	Maury Muehleisen	Plane crash
1974	Nick Drake	Drug overdose
1974	Momma Cass	Heart attack
1974	Dave Alexander	Illness
1975	Tim Buckley	Drug overdose
1975	Peter Ham	Suicide
1976	Tommy Bolin	Drug overdose
1976	Keith Relf	Electrocution
1977	Marc Bolan	Car accident

1977	Ronnie Van Zant	Plane crash
1977	Steve Gaines	Plane crash
1977	Cassie Gaines	Plane crash
1978	Terry Kath	Shooting
1978	Keith Moon	Drug overdose
1978	Chris Bell	Car accident
1978	Nancy Spungen	Murder
1978	Barry Brown	Suicide
1979	Jimmy McCulloch	Drug overdose
1979	Sid Vicious	Suicide
1979	John Glascock	Illness
1980	John Lennon	Murder
1980	John Bonham	Illness
1980	Tommy Caldwell	Car accident
1980	Carl Radle	Illness
1981	Bob Marley	Illness
1981	Harry Chapin	Car accident
1982	James Scott	Drug overdose
1983	Karen Carpenter	Heart attack
1983	Pete Farndon	Drug overdose
1983	Felix Pappalardi	Shooting
1983	Tom Evans	Suicide
1983	Dennis Wilson	Drowning
1984	Marvin Gaye	Shooting

There are those among us who will downplay such talk as mere fantasy and seek to "explain away" this information, which is entirely their prerogative. Hey, if they want to believe in the tooth fairy - let them.

But what cannot be "explained away" is the fact that every cover-up in the murder of Elvis Presley followed the same formula that ran through the entertainment and political landscape beginning in the 1950s and continuing well into the 1980s.

The cover-up of the Elvis Presley, John Kennedy, Sonny Liston and Marilyn Monroe murders were nearly identical – hastily cleaned and staged crime scenes, yet no one apparently gave the order to clean them.

The following four quotes are from network TV's *JFK: Inside the Target Car.*

> "Then an unnamed secret service agent asked Parkland personnel to clean the limo interior." "One of the really strange stories about Parkland Hospital has to do with a bucket sitting next to the Kennedy limousine and apparently the Secret Service cleaning out part of the interior. The car, of course, is a crime scene and here is someone altering the crime scene. Is he sweeping up evidence? What's he doing? We don't know!"

> "In the chaos that followed no one stopped to evaluate the forensic evidence left in the limo." "As soon as the press saw Kennedy's car and no one in it and the emergency entrance sign above it, they knew there was a big story. They didn't know what it was but they knew they had to cover it and they started getting pictures and what they wanted were picture inside the

> limousine, and they went up toward the car and the Secret Service kept them all back – pushed them back and they made no bones about it."

Now compare the quotes above describing the odd cleanup of President Kennedy's crime scene with the following three quotes from Thompson and Cole's *The Death of Elvis;*

> "Warlick's thoughts were elsewhere. He was suspicious of the sparkling bathroom, the general sanitized smell of it, and the absence of drugs. And Warlick still found clues there, despite the efforts to hide them." "Warlick turned to Esposito and Strada and asked, 'Had he vomited? Are there any specimens? Is this exactly how it was when you found him?' 'No,' Esposito replied. 'The maid's been in here and cleaned up."
>
> "Jones recalled what the bathroom looked like when he and his partner went back for their (EMT) equipment. 'Everything, everything had been cleaned up. The bed had been made, the rest of the room and everything had been cleaned up. Our equipment was placed over on the sink in a neat pile.'"

It's more than obvious that in both situations, someone had been charged with the responsibility of altering the crime scene before the true evidence could have been analyzed and a thorough murder investigation launched.

This isn't a blind coincidence. Consider the following parallels and planted evidence with the intent to throw professional investigators off the track. The book *Ultimate Sacrifice* by Lamar Waldron and Thom Hartmann states the following,

> "At about 1:45, Parkland Hospital senior engineer Darrell Tomlinson found the nearly pristine bullet. It was on one of two stretchers close together in a hallway, one of which had probably been used to transport Connally, while the other hadn't been used for either Kennedy or Connally. Both stretchers had probably been unattended for thirty minutes, in a hall with various people about. Regardless of who placed the pristine bullet on the stretcher, it was used to link Oswald's rifle to the shooting of JFK and Connally."

Now consider the planting of the drug syringes in Elvis Presley's murder – syringes that had no needles in them, and were found in locations designed to absorb the investigator's attention and distract the medical examiner from probing a murder.

There's also a stunning similarity between Elvis Presley's death and the death of former heavyweight champion Sonny Liston. During the US government's removal of Muhammad Ali's boxing title for his refusal to be enlisted for the Vietnam draft, Liston had the opportunity to become heavyweight champion once again by defeating Chuck Wepner.

It was reported by Liston himself that he had been approached two days before his fight by two Las Vegas mobsters who were betting heavily on Liston losing. Liston ignored the mobster's demands to take a dive and beat Wepner so badly that he needed 54 stitches in his face.

Within days of Liston winning the fight he was found dead. The official cause of death was a "suspected" drug overdose, but Liston wasn't a drug user. Three heroin packets were found in plain view on the kitchen counter, a small amount of marijuana was found in his pocket, along with a syringe on the bed.

He was found badly bloated and decomposed, wearing only a T-shirt with foam coming from his mouth and a trickle of blood coming from his nose. At least three hours had elapsed between when the body was discovered and when the police were called, and the explanation for the time lapse was murky at best.

The coroner claimed there were not enough drugs in his liver to warrant a drug death. The official cause of death was listed as *"cardiac arrhythmia"* – a stopped heart. Sound familiar?

In the video series *The Mysterious Life and Death of a Champion*, Dean Weideman, former Las Vegas police sergeant explains,

> *"There was far too many hours passed between the time that Mrs. Liston entered the house and found the body and when the actual call was made to our department. Time to remove things,*

> to change things, where was the surgical tubing that he would have probably used to wrap around his arm to expose a vein? Where was the spoon used for cooking? Had it been moved? None of this stuff was present, and of course, you know, the lack of things can be as suspicious as actual items of evidence there."

At the autopsy there were needle marks in his arm, but everyone who knew Liston, including his dentist, knew that he was deathly afraid of needles. Like the mysterious murders and crime scene cleanings of JFK, Sonny Liston and Elvis Presley, one must take into evidence the death of Marilyn Monroe.

Monroe's death was also mysteriously cleaned and the findings at the death scene seemed to defy both logic and science. Sgt. Jack Clemmons was noted describing what he saw upon his arrival at the scene:

> "Marilyn was lying face down in what I call the soldier's position. Her hands were by her side and her legs were stretched out perfectly straight. It was the most obviously staged death scene I have ever seen. The pill bottles on her bedside table had been arranged in neat order and the body deliberately positioned. It all looked too tidy."

Clemmons was correct in his assumption that something was very suspicious, but there wouldn't be a comprehensive investigation.

No one knew exactly who Marilyn Monroe called on her last night, because the telephone records have vanished without so much as one telephone company employee knowing how.

However, Marilyn was overheard talking on the telephone by her maid as she walked by her door and the last person she called was President Kennedy.

Dr. Thomas Noguchi, who has been heralded as L.A.'s *'Coroner to the Stars'* claimed that evidence samples were missing and that the police investigation at the death scene had been so tainted by sloppy police work that it was impossible to give a clear cause of the star's death.

Much like the sloppy work of the Dallas Police Department in the JFK murder in 1963, and Presley's murder in 1977. Apparently the sloppiness didn't improve when Monroe's body was delivered to the morgue as standard procedures were ignored.

Typically when a body is brought into the morgue an inspection by medical staff for bruises, cuts, and other trauma are routinely outlined on an initial examination form which begins the official file of the autopsy.

In Monroe's case, the initial examination form, the autopsy file, and all of the medical examinations findings were lost, with the exception of one page, one single page. The same single page they filled out in Elvis' autopsy.

However, Noguchi did come up with some "off the cuff" conclusions that were quite startling. He noted that according to the position of the body Marilyn Monroe's death scene was obviously staged.

He noted that because blood pools at the lowest level of the body when the heart stops after as little as 3 hours and it produces purple blotching on the skin, a process known as "livor mortis", this purple blotching was on the wrong side of Marilyn's face from the position she was found in.

Obviously the body had been moved and repositioned, a fact immediately noticed by Sgt. Jack Clemmons. The questions are: Why, and by whom? In post mortem more questions were raised.

The remaining autopsy diagram clearly contains the notation "No needle marks," but according to an invoice submitted to Monroe's estate by her doctor, he claimed that he had injected her personally.

These injections were done the night before her death – why were they not found on her body? The growing parallels between these odd deaths and their connection to the mob and Elvis Presley's death are far beyond coincidental; they are obvious, stark and glaring.

Consider the departure from logical autopsy procedures in the murders of Elvis Presley, Marilyn Monroe, and President Kennedy. Marilyn Monroe's coroner stated that she died from an oral overdose of Nembutal and chloral hydrate, swallowing 50 pills at once. But there was no yellow-dye discoloration on the lining of the intestine that normally occurs in such cases, impossible for pills that have a street name of "Yellow Jackets".

There was no evidence that partially or completely undissolved capsules entered her digestive tract. The scarcity of evidence was shocking, as all specimens of tissue samples from the corpse had oddly vanished, much like Elvis' stomach contents that were mysteriously rinsed down the drain in the ER.

The official photos taken at Monroe's death scene have been "lost" – much like the photos of the Presley death scene that were stolen out of Dan Warlick's car the same night Elvis died.

This is covered in *The Death of Elvis*: *"That night Dan Warlick's car was burglarized, and the small spiral pad he used to take notes at Graceland and in the autopsy room was stolen."*

In the book, Warlick seemed to think that the thief didn't know the value of the stolen information as it has never emerged for sale; it's not shocking at all, profit was not their intention - silence was.

Warlick's information and all of his photos needed to vanish! In the Presley autopsy, cameras were present by procedure in the autopsy room to take face shots for identification purposes, but none were taken. The medical examiner actually ignored his own policies and procedures by not taking photos. Why?

To this day no photos of the Presley autopsy or the Graceland investigation exist anywhere. How is this possible? In the autopsy of President Kennedy, the photos taken do not match the side head wound that the Zapruder film shows.

The following photo is the frame of the Zapruder film that shows the face of President Kennedy being torn from his head. You can even see the scalp being thrown back towards the First Lady's face with his entire jaw and sinus cavity exposed. Further, you can clearly see that flesh and gray matter hang deeply into the Presidents lap and his right eye appears to be missing!

Photo by Robert Groden

This is what the *real* Zapruder film shows. How do I know this is the real version? I am friends with the guy who brought it over from France where it was originally being stored.

This, the real version of the film, looks nothing like the numerous altered copies that have been reworked using computer-generated imagery (CGI) technology in order to promote the government's agenda.

The phony CGI copies are easy to find, all you have to do is go on the web and search for them. They are almost as phony as JFK's public domain autopsy photo that our government has released. They are also easily found, in fact one of them is shown here.

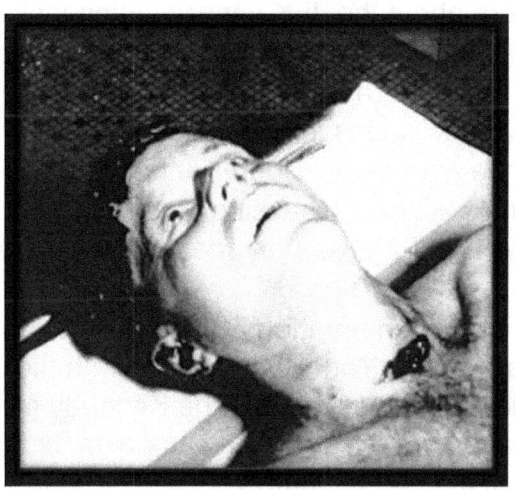

After seeing this photo we must ask ourselves how did the President's face magically regenerate itself? Look at the two photos. How is this possible? The only logical answer is a quart of morticians wax and a tremendous amount of effort. Why?

I am not a big conspiracy guy, and I really don't want to believe that they happen, but if more than two people were involved in this JFK photo fraud than we must call it was it is. It aligns perfectly with the legal definition of Conspiracy.

Obviously the American people were never supposed to see the Zapruder film and the autopsy photo was conveniently contorted by the government to sell us on the single bullet theory, a theory that defies both the laws of physics and the laws of ballistics.

For more about the JFK assassination look for my upcoming book, *Who Murdered JFK?* In that book I pick apart the obvious cracks of the JFK assassination and I deliver my conclusions in a very common-sense way. The defense attorney for John Kennedy and Martin Luther King's alleged assassins, Lee Harvey Oswald and James Earl Ray, was my friend, Mark Lane.

Quite more than an attorney, Mr. Lane was elected in 1960 to the New York State Senate with the support of both Eleanor Roosevelt and the Kennedy family. He then managed JFK's New York campaign for his presidential bid and became very close friends with the president as well as his brother, Bobby.

After the assassination of the President, Lane worked feverishly to disprove the lone-gunman theory with facts that the US government had intentionally overlooked and hid from the public with its Warren Commission Report.

He did so in his two best-selling books – *Rush to Judgment* and *Plausible Denial*. Unfortunately, the world lost Mark on May 10th 2016. Mark lived to the ripe old age of 89 and died of natural causes, which was no easy feat as he was constantly on the government's radar.

I had known Mark for many years and finally had the luxury of meeting him in person. Our face-to-face meeting happened on October 18th 2013 at the Cyril H. Wecht institute at Duquesne University in Pittsburgh Pa.

Dr. Wecht was hosting an International Symposium to commemorate the 50th Anniversary of the Assassination of President John F. Kennedy. Myself, Dr. Wecht, Mark Lane, and filmmaker Oliver Stone were joined by a host of leading scientific, legal and investigative experts on the Kennedy murder.

Every one of the 150 people at Dr. Wecht's symposium along with the rest of the world owes Mark a huge debt of gratitude. If it wasn't for his tireless efforts and his continuous badgering of governmental leaders combined with his keen use of the Freedom of Information Act (FOIA), we still wouldn't have seen the Zapruder film.

In it took twelve long years of internal pressure for the government to release this film, and when they did release it, the frame just before impact, showing the bullet trajectory, was mysteriously "lost." What a surprise. The medical evidence pointing to the cause of death that was given in both the Elvis Presley and Dr. Martin Luther King Jr. murders was, to say the least, highly suspect. Both men were murdered in the City of Memphis, Tennessee, and both autopsies were handled by Medical Examiner, Jerry T. Francisco.

In 1968, Francisco failed to dissect Martin Luther King's fatal gunshot wound, which made it impossible for the panel of experts to confirm that shots were fired from the boarding-house window.

The trajectory wasn't documented correctly, and the shot could have come from a clump of bushes on the street level where witnesses noticed movement. The following are copyrighted excerpts from Mark Lane's book *Murder in Memphis.* Upon viewing my research he has granted me one time use of the following information in order to elaborate my point.

Mr. Lane writes:

> "Francisco said that the bullet had angled downward from right to left passing through the chin, the base of the neck, and the spinal cord into the back. Francisco offered the opinion that the angle of the bullet through the body was consistent with a shot having been fired from the rooming house." "Francisco did not state that he knew where Dr. King had been standing, which direction he had been facing, or if he had been leaning over when he was shot, thereby considerably reducing the value of his opinion as to the origin of the shot."

In 1977, uncovered evidence clearly refutes Francisco's cause of death as Dr. Florendo disputes that Elvis' death was heart related. In fact Florendo clearly stated on camera that he was surprised at Francisco's announcement as he saw no "gross evidence" of a heart attack.

The Shelby County Medical Examiner, Dr. Jerry T. Francisco, was a seasoned veteran of the autopsy and forensic trenches and there was simply no way he could have made errors such as these. Francisco graduated from the University of Tennessee Health Science Center in 1955 and took up residence at both City of Memphis Hospitals in 1960, and the Institute of Pathology for the University of Tennessee in 1963.

He began his tenure as the Shelby County Medical Examiner beginning in 1961, taking on all varieties of autopsy and investigative cases with swift professionalism. Botching autopsies of such high-profile figures as Elvis Presley and Dr. Martin Luther King, Jr. had to be intentional or instructed by higher authorities, as were the altered autopsy photos of JFK.

Consider further the lost files of the Marilyn Monroe autopsy. The same is true regarding the death of Martin Luther King, Jr. – a man who wanted nothing but peace and justice who was murdered by hired government operatives. Again, like Oswald, James Earl Ray was made to suffer the role of the patsy. Mark Lane was the legal counsel for Mr. Ray and wrote in *Murder in Memphis*:

> "No fingerprints or palm prints placed Ray in the rooming house and indeed those that were located seemed to point in another direction which evidently was not explored by police. No evidence demonstrated that Ray's rifle had fired the bullet which struck Dr. King and there, too, the evidence appeared to point in another direction which apparently the police also failed to examine."

In all the world there was only one eyewitness who could have testified to Ray's innocence and her name was Grace Stephens. Time after time she positively identified the shooter, and it was not James Earl Ray.

To suppress this information, the authorities swiftly had the woman committed to a mental hospital under an assumed name in an attempt to permanently sequester, sedate, and discredit her testimony from ever going public.

Mark Lane writes:

> "Yet she was illegally placed in a mental institution by the Tennessee authorities soon after the assassination. When Hays sought to question her, she was transferred to another institution under a different name. We found her on November 12 at the institution in Bolivar, where she was confined under the name Grace Waldon."

"Just after Grace Stephens told me that she believed that her husband had not seen the man who murdered Dr. King, a man in charge of the building at the institution and a woman employee of the institution approached me. The woman, who identified herself, only after my repeated request that she do so, as Daisy Cox, said, 'You cannot talk to Grace.'"

The appalling treatment of James Earl Ray when imprisoned in the Shelby County jail directly led to his mental and physical deterioration. A deterioration that was so stark that after just a handful of weeks he pled guilty to get it over with.

Mark Lane from his book *Murder in Memphis*:

"Ray was imprisoned in the Shelby County Jail in Memphis in maximum security until he pleaded guilty. During the months he was jailed, bright lights were kept on him twenty-four hours each day."

"Closed circuit cameras monitored his every move. Guards were present in the cell with him while other guards watched him from the other side of the bars. Microphones in the cell picked up and magnified every sound that he made. Even his breathing was heard. Months later when Ray described the conditions in the cell during a civil suit against Foreman and Huie, he testified, 'As I stated, maximum security jail, lights on twenty-four hours a day, steel plates *over the windows, two television sets watching me all the time...no fresh air."*

"Two months after Hanes had appealed to Judge Battle for some relief from the oppressive jail conditions, Michael Eugene, an English solicitor who had been appointed to represent Ray's rights in London, saw Ray. He was astonished by the deterioration in Ray's condition. He said that Ray looked sick, weak and nervous. When James Earl Ray pleaded guilty, a reporter from the Chicago Daily News interviewed his brother, John Ray. John said that he had doubted that his brother would plead guilty but that the strain of being under constant observation in his cell by guards and closed circuit television must have affected him."

Suppressing the truth has become an art form in these types of situations, especially in the murder of Elvis Presley and Dr. Martin Luther King Jr. Even if the officials in Memphis had publicly admitted that Presley was murdered and launched an actual investigation, the person arrested for the deed would have been a fall guy innocently selected from Presley's inner circle of family and friends.

In fact, the "Patsy Syndrome" was so obvious to Dr. King's widow that neither she nor Dr. King's heirs believe that James Earl Ray was guilty of the murder. In a Washington Post article titled *"The War over King's Legacy,"* written by Vern E. Smith and Jon Meacham, the authors write the following:

> "Now, 30 years after his assassination, that legend is under fresh assault – from King's own family and many of his aging lieutenants. His widow, Coretta, and his heirs are on the front lines of a quiet but pitched battle over the manner of his death and the meaning of his life. They believe James Earl Ray, King's convicted assassin, is innocent and that history has forgotten the real Martin Luther King."

Just as all effort and investigation in Memphis seemed to elude officials in the Presley murder, that same zone of illegality extended to the whole of Shelby County Tennessee. Apparently at that time period in the nation's midriff not only did motivation for an official criminal investigation take a holiday, but so did most of the rights and amendments of the United States Constitution.

It's obvious that the King murder was just another government-designed assassination, and like Elvis Presley's murder, the weight of the evidence that could have pointed to the truth was never revealed.

This seems to coincide with the general consensus of Presley's Memphis Mafia, as a startling statement is made by Dick Grob and Sam Thompson in *The Death of Elvis.* Both men believed that they would have a better chance keeping a drug death or any other scandal quiet in Memphis than in any other city in the United States of America – why?

Obviously they knew that Francisco could be controlled from within. The same *Memphis Magic* that could cover up a scandal if the circumstances warranted it was used by Colonel Parker as the ultimate back stage pass. Anything he wanted, anywhere he wanted it, was made possible for Parker.

The myth that Parker was a promotional genie and mystical star maker couldn't have been farther from the truth; he just played the mob powers like a xylophone and was smart enough to always give them a cut of the action.

That is the ultimate show of respect and the perfect way to ensure a long-lasting business relationship. Sure, Colonel Parker cashed Elvis' paychecks, but his true client was the mob, where people in the highest of places gave him anything that he wanted.

Parker's cut went from 25% of Presley's take to 50% in 1967 and far beyond in the last years of Presley's life. There's a now-famous interview with Colonel Parker's assistant, Byron Raphael, at *ClassicBands.com* in which Raphael sheds light on the Colonel Parker who existed behind the stage, and the scale of the Colonel's thievery to feed his gambling habit.

Raphael explains:

> "...*the last five or six years, it, (Parker's take) wasn't 50%, but more like 80% or 90%...As a matter of fact, William Morris never had a*

contract, the Colonel never signed a contract with William Morris. Yet, he paid them a commission on everything – even after Elvis died. By the way, Elvis made more money when he was dead than when he was alive. It was amazing. The Colonel's tenacity and nerve was unbelievable."

As far back in Presley's career as 1967, toward the end of his movie career, Parker spelled out RCA's mob involvement. Parker told Presley exactly what the mob expected Elvis to do, and how they expected him to behave. Becoming a government agent wasn't on that list.

Nor was providing cover in Las Vegas for agents to investigate the mob while staying in mob-run hotels. Also not on the list was turning witness against the mob in his airplane fraud case, or trying to reveal the hidden truth behind the JFK assassination.

Colonel Tom Parker, with his dubious connections, made it very clear to Presley who was pulling the strings, and that Presley needed to behave himself. Alanna Nash in *The Colonel* explains how Sam Cooke was killed.

Parker explained to Elvis that the real killer wasn't the manager of a hotel as the media reported; the mob killed him because he was stepping out of line and wouldn't shut up when he was warned.

"Word came down and the hit was made. The mob wasn't gangsters in the street anymore, Parker explained. It was heads of corporations like RCA, the East Coast, Sicilian families – men whose last names ended in vowels, men with uncles called Jimmy 'The Thumb.' Colonel told Elvis, 'You've got to behave yourself. You can only go so far,' says Larry Geller. And Elvis knew the Colonel was a dangerous enemy."

Still, a tiny group of people refuse to believe that Elvis Presley died on August 16th 1977. They support their longstanding belief by claiming that the government placed Elvis in a witness protection plan, or that he faked his own death to escape the rigors of the entertainment world.

While most of the *Elvis Is Alive* phenomena is a smattering of conjecture and hogwash, a trace amount of evidence has been discovered that would indicate the possibility.

For example, there were two death certificates filed. One was filed by the Shelby County Medical Examiner, and the other by Elvis' personal physician Dr. George Nichopolous.

A Presley family member advised Elvis researcher, Gail Brewer Giorgio, to investigate the handwriting on the second death certificate. After an exhaustive investigation in which Paul Weist, a criminal graphologist specializing in forgeries, confirmed that Elvis Presley had indeed completed his own death certificate.

These are facts; however, this isn't the smoking gun that everyone might assume. US Government agents have long planted evidence like this to sway the public's perception. If you remember from earlier in the chapter, this was one of the main functions of the COINTELPRO program, to plant false paperwork and evidence.

In the JFK murder, the planting of the pristine bullet on the stretcher was designed to "wag the dog", so to speak, in the opposite direction of a presidential assassination conspiracy.

Like the empty drug syringes planted at Graceland, there's no better way to draw the eyes of investigation and public opinion away from reality of murder than to plant confusing and abstract evidence.

Take for example the planted drugs at the murder scene of Sonny Liston – a man who was outspoken against the nation's drug culture.

All a professional assassin needs is planted evidence to sway the media into believing the murder was something else. When planted drugs are found, the death suddenly becomes a drug death, and all thoughts of a murder vanish.

Consider the stories of the witnesses who have changed their minds, and continue to change them, through the years. The whole premise of the ever-changing storyline, the planting of evidence and the muddling of facts were controlled unknowingly by Joe Esposito through a man pulling his strings from thousands of miles away – Colonel Parker. Parker organized the murder with his mob connections which produced gigantic profits from the after-death merchandising and record sales. The Colonel played it perfectly. Before Presley's death he had approached Vernon Presley to set up a company to handle the merchandising of Elvis's nonperformance products, souvenir products, new music publishing companies, and basically total control of Elvis Presley's commercial rights and image.

This was done legally with Elvis receiving a cut of the take which was badly slanted in Parker's favor. Parker received a whopping 56% of the profits to the 22% that Presley and Parker's assistant and president of Boxcar Enterprises, Tom Diskin, received.

In other words: Elvis Presley was worth more money dead than alive. Elvis' image doesn't tire, get sick, talk back to the Colonel, or behave unpredictably on stage, and since Elvis' tours and records were no longer selling at the record clip like they had previously, Colonel Parker had just found his new cash cow. "Boxcar" was a curious name for his enterprise, but one that I am sure he was very familiar.

How else would an illegal alien with no money travel through America, most likely stowing away in a Boxcar. It fits. Parker knew that if he had approached Elvis personally he would have hit a brick wall, so the old carny pitched the idea to the one person that Elvis totally trusted – Vernon.

In no time, Vernon convinced Elvis that his estate needed the funds and with a few strokes of the pen, Boxcar Enterprises became the sole entity through which "all things Presley" would be sold.

What the Colonel pitched to Vernon was a little contract so everyone could make some extra money on the side. That certainly was not the case.
In reality, Vernon hadn't signed a merchandising contract; he signed his son's death warrant.

Byron Raphael, the Colonel's assistant is quoted as saying the following in Nash's book: *"The real deadliness of Colonel Parker was that he believed the living Elvis had become an impediment to his management style and ambition."* This quote explains Parker's mindset and all but spells out who the killer would be.

Colonel Parker owed millions to major players in the underworld through his gambling debts and they were no longer waiting patiently for repayment. Parker feared for his own life, or a fate that he deemed worse than death itself, the exposure of his murderous past and illegal alien status to the media.

This massive extortion of Presley's money was so severe that Priscilla was shocked at how little Elvis actually had in his bank accounts after his death. Elvis Presley was a worldwide phenomenon and had sold billions of records in his lifetime.

He had cashed paychecks worth multiple millions of dollars – where the hell did all the money go?! The more Parker satisfied his gambling compulsion in Las Vegas, the more the mob could squeeze him for a greater percentage of his wages and the more he ran Elvis into sickness and exhaustion.

No wonder there is so much footage of Elvis Presley performing badly in the mid-1970s; they all but had a gun to his head to keep him performing, and if Elvis didn't perform date after date at breakneck speed Parker couldn't pay up, and if Parker couldn't pay up, the story of his illegal immigrant status would have been leaked to every major news station in the world.

If that information was leaked it would have meant Parker's rapid deportation and a murder prosecution in the Netherlands. Elvis, on the other hand, was expendable, and if the murder was done properly, even more money could be made. A dead Elvis was the best option for everyone involved.

Parker knew that Elvis was in poor health and that his medical problems were mounting. He also knew that as sickly and bloated as Elvis had looked in his last few years most people wouldn't ask many questions when he ended up dead, but waiting for him to die at some point down the road would have meant waiting too long for Parker.

The Colonel needed to act fast. To decode the complete fabrication of Presley's last night on earth was to wade through endless odds and ends of banter totally disassociated with fact.

By all accounts, at 4:00am, a racquetball game begins between Elvis, Ginger, Billy Smith and Jo Smith. During this racquetball odyssey the four players switched teams and played for over an hour. Already there are problems in this story, and Elvis is hours away from death.

During the autopsy, Dr. Noel Florendo performed a procedure called *"running the gut,"* where a doctor takes a flat-billed pair of surgical scissors and cuts the five - to seven - foot colon and large intestine lengthwise to reveal and analyze its contents.

This is a common autopsy procedure. It's a job that no one really wants to do but it needs to be done. The procedure is usually uneventful; however, in the case of Elvis Presley, it became quite telling.

Dr. Florendo discovered that Elvis' megacolon was jam packed with hardened white fecal matter to the point where his colon was stretched far beyond the normal 2 inches. Incredibly Elvis' colon was stretched to a whopping 5 inches. This was unheard of.

According to Dr. Florendo, Elvis must have been in misery as he hadn't had a bowel movement in nearly three weeks. There's no way Elvis Presley, or any man who is compacted with several feet of claylike fecal matter, would have the desire, or the ability, to play racquetball for any length of time, let alone the hour that is suggested.

Billy Smith is interviewed as saying that Elvis hit his shin with the racquet, which resulted in a welt that ended the game. This is covered in the DVD, *Elvis: The Last 24 Hours,* but this is impossible, as there was no sign of this injury during Dan Warlick's autopsy inspection of the corpse.

Since the autopsy results are a physical fact and the racquetball game is hearsay, the evidence indicates that this racquetball game could not have happened. So what's the real story?

Billy Smith's story continues to say that after the racquetball game, Elvis sat at the piano in the lounge area of the racquetball building playing and singing songs, and then retired to his bedroom where he needed Billy Smith to wash his hair.

Exactly why Elvis was able to play a racquetball marathon but couldn't manage to wash and dry his own hair, requiring Billy Smith walking an eighth-mile out of his way to do so, is totally out of balance with reality.

This is significant for numerous reasons: First, there's no real account of Presley's whereabouts during the predawn hours of 4:00am through 7:00am. Second, these people are lying. Why? What are they trying so hard to cover up?

To further the story of Elvis' last night, at 7:00am Elvis and Ginger retire to the bed. Ginger alleges that at 9:30am Elvis was restless and unable to sleep. In an interview Ginger stated that:

"He took his book on psychic energy with him and he started toward the bathroom door, and I said, 'Now don't fall asleep,' and he turned and smiled at me and said, "Okay, I won't."'

This is the story that Ginger has repeated many times over the years and in many interviews without exception. Unfortunately, it's a fantasy. When questioned by Dan Warlick, she couldn't correctly name the book Elvis was reading, even though she claimed she saw him pick up the book and head for the bathroom to read it. This is more than a curious development.

Adding to this, she also reported that Elvis smiled at her as he left the bedroom. This is also a curious statement, as the room had to be dark. It's well known that Presley was nocturnal and slept during the day, and to accommodate him the windows to his upstairs lair had been blacked out years prior.

Ginger couldn't have it both ways. Either she told the truth when she said that she saw Elvis smile at her to read because the lights were on, or she couldn't have seen the title of the book because the lights were off.

Here we have a girl who's sleeping with a man who is an avid reader and she can't remember what book he is reading? Furthermore, she claimed that she was sleeping when Elvis got up to read. Was she sleeping with the lights on? Why haven't the police asked these questions? Why haven't the police asked **_ANY_** questions?

Ginger's story of discovering Elvis didn't add up either. Dan Warlick reported that Ginger had Elvis falling out of a chair and not off the toilet. Further, she told the police that Presley's body was slumped to one side and his head was against the wall. Again, that was not factual.

Due to these odd inconsistencies and variations, there's no way Ginger Alden was with Elvis Presley when he died or she would have known better. Ginger alleges that at approximately 9:30am Elvis got out of bed and went into the bathroom to read.

This is impossible as the doctors had determined the time of death at around 9:30am Also, Elvis signed Paul Lichter's special delivery letter at 9:30am. Further adding to the mystery of Ginger's whereabouts is the lonely call Elvis made to his nurse and close friend Marion Cocke.

In an undated and unidentified YouTube video Ms. Cocke told the camera that she received a 9:00am phone call from Elvis asking if she would stop by and keep him company until "plane time" as he was supposed to fly out of town to begin his tour. This is something that she typically did because she was a nice woman who loved spending to time with Elvis.

However, if someone is lonely and calls for company, logic would dictate that they are, indeed, alone. So where was Ginger at 9:00am when Elvis called Ms. Cocke? Or a better question: where was Ginger at 9:30am, the time when the coroner estimated his death? Where ever she was, she wasn't with Elvis.

Billy Smith, Elvis' cousin, claimed that he was first notified of Elvis's death at *"1:30 or a quarter to 2,"* which doesn't align with the EMTs documents or any other account of any witness.

David Stanley changed his story so many times you have to struggle to follow it. By his many accounts, when he discovered that Presley was dead, he smuggled someone out of Graceland in his car at a high rate of speed.

In the 1980 Stanley brothers book *Elvis, We Love You Tender*, he claimed that the man in the car was Mark White. Six years later in 1986 he released another book, *Life with Elvis*, and claimed that Elvis' cousin Billy Smith was the passenger. In 1989, three years later, he told Geraldo Rivera that Elvis' death had to have been accidental because Elvis didn't believe in suicide.

One year later, on Geraldo Rivera's popular TV show, he claimed that Elvis did commit suicide. Are you following this? No? Neither could anyone else. David Stanley's dalliances and deviations from the truth are well covered in John Parker's book *Elvis - Murdered by the Mob*.

Parker writes:

"In his first book, he said he came on duty late on the morning of the sixteenth, bringing a friend named Mark White to the Graceland to play pool." "The second book went through much the same detail, though made no mention of the

friend named Mark, or of delivering him out of the estate grounds before going up to see what was wrong with Elvis. Members of the entourage have often speculated on the identity of this man, and were even more mystified later still when, in 1990, David Stanley claimed that Elvis committed suicide and he had helped destroy the evidence that pointed to it."

Clearly everyone is telling tall tales but when it comes to the holy grail of fabrication one must stand in awe of Joe Esposito. Immediately after the news broke that Presley was dead, Joe Esposito, accompanied by Charlie Hodge, gave the following video interview to a reporter at Baptist Memorial Hospital.

Esposito: "Well, he was upstairs in the bedroom, and I went upstairs to talk to him and he wasn't breathing when I got there."

Reporter: Was he lying on the bed?

Esposito: Yeah.

Reporter: Were there any signs of ill health?

Esposito: None whatsoever. "

Two hours later at Graceland, he told investigator Dan Warlick Elvis had fallen off the toilet. Then he claimed in later interviews that he called 911 from Presley's toilet-side phone, at a time when 911 didn't exist in Memphis. Variations of his twisted storyline have also grown to include giving Presley mouth-to-mouth resuscitation and moving the body from the bedroom to the bathroom floor. Finally, his story evolved to his most recent admission, covered in the DVD *The Day Elvis Died*, in which he stated:

> *"I go into the bathroom and see Elvis on the floor. He fell off the commode. His face was buried in the carpeting, and I bend down real quick and I touched him and rigor mortis had set in, and I turned him over real quick and pulled up his pajama bottoms."*
>
> *"I turned him over and laid down and I heard a little breath of air come out of his lungs, so I thought maybe he was going to be okay, but I just didn't feel comfortable about it. I grabbed the phone real quick – there was a phone on the wall right next to the commode."*
>
> *"I called 911 and told them we need an ambulance at Graceland so get someone here quick, and then Al picked up the phone and tried to get Dr. Nick while I was trying to...now there's a story that says I gave Elvis mouth-to-mouth resuscitation. I did not give Elvis mouth-to-mouth resuscitation. You couldn't. His mouth was closed shut and there was no way I could open his mouth. But I tried to massage his heart."*

In other interviews Joe Esposito claimed that he colored the grey out of Presley's temples as his regrowth between tours was obvious. This claim was later changed in the 1980's as Esposito claimed that Charlie Hodge colored Presley's hair.

Thirty years after the fact in the DVD *Elvis: The Last 24 Hours,* Larry Geller, Presley's personal hair stylist told that camera that he was asked by Presley's father Vernon to tend to Presley's hair and that he blended Elvis's grey re-growth out with black mascara that one of the female morticians had.

Other clues that something was amiss came in reading the fact-loaded book *The Death of Elvis*. The following four quotes are extremely important to unlock the true suppression of evidence in the Presley murder:

1. "Florendo said he could not find enough evidence to substantiate cardiac arrhythmia." (Pg. 177)

2. "... failed to write down the weight on the form." (Pg. 45)

3. "He seemed small in death." (Pg. 44)

4. "Although it was standard procedure in the Shelby County Medical Examiner's Office to take face shots of the subject before an autopsy, he took no photographs." (Pg.44)

Could it be any more obvious why everyone is lying or breaking from their normal procedures? Everyone is being "strong armed". Clearly all common procedures for identifying the body were ignored.

As in all government-spawned conspiracies, someone must suppress the dangerous knowledge and keep it from reaching the public. All the loose ends must be trimmed and replaced with disinformation.

The government is good at this because it has had a lot of practice. Just as Mark Lane had uncovered the witness to the shooting of Dr. Martin Luther King that the US government had silenced by admitting her to a mental hospital under an assumed name to conceal the truth that James Earl Ray was not the shooter, legendary researcher Jim Marrs had done the same with Kennedy assassination.

Marrs, who died only a few months after Lane, departed this world a few weeks before we were scheduled to meet and discuss his JFK assassination facts. It was the worst possible time for me to lose both of them as I was right in the middle of my research for the third volume in this series, *Who Murdered JFK?*.

I was so looking forward to speaking with Jim about his list of people who were mysteriously murdered after the JFK assassination. Marrs' list was entitled *Strange and Convenient Deaths Surrounding the Assassination.* There he reveals the level that the US government had gone to silence those with information that could work contrary to their lone gunman narrative that they were so eager to push.

First on that list was the November 1963 murder of Karyn Kupcinet. Kupcinet was the daughter of Irving Kupcinet, a syndicated columnist with the *Chicago Sun-Times* who would later replace NBC's TV legend Jack Parr. Irv was a twenty-year friend of Jack Ruby and the two men remained in close contact.

Karyn was a budding young actress who received information that JFK was going to be assassinated through her father and was murdered after trying to place a long distance telephone call to the White House.

According to the long distance operator she heard Kupcinet scream into the telephone that President Kennedy was going to be killed. She was forever silenced and paid the price with her life. Last on the list was the murder of Roy Kellerman in March of 1984.

Kellerman was in charge of JFK's secret service detail and supplied concrete evidence to the Warren Commission proving conspiracy but the commission ignored his evidence and his in-depth testimony.

Kellerman died mysteriously as he was becoming more and more vocal about the secret service failures that day in Dallas and he became a more frequent guest on television demanding that something be done about it.

All totaled there were 104 people that Jim Marrs had painstakingly compiled from 1963 to 1984. Everyone on the list had evidence, was a witness to, or had intimate knowledge of the conspiracy to murder President Kennedy and each and every one of them had been murdered or died mysteriously. The odds of over one hundred people being connected with the assassination either being murdered or dying in the most bizarre circumstances would be so high that it simply couldn't be calculated.

No one in any Las Vegas sports book would even attempt to handicap the odds. They would have to be twenty trillion to one. It would be impossible for that to just "happen."

Could there be any more proof positive that LBJ's best friend and neighbor, J. Edgar Hoover, was running his COINTELPRO project to the letter? Accompanying the silencing of witnesses to the JFK and MLK assassinations would be the mysterious deaths in the aftermath of the Presley murder.

Immediately after Presley's death, his private doctor, Dr. Nichopolous, was nearly killed by a bullet when he and an associate were attending a local football game.

The good doctor was sitting in the stands and was suddenly struck in the chest, center mass, with a bullet that surely would have killed him instantly if its power hadn't been depleted from being shot from such a long distance.

Instead of having half of his chest blown out by the intended assassination the bullet merely pierced Nichopolous' jacket and left a welt falling to the ground. Why was the doctor such a target?

Dr. Nichopolous had been steeped in the knowledge that Elvis Presley's death was not natural and was assisting Vernon Presley with his attempts to get the Memphis Police Department to investigate the facts of the murder.

Similar knowledge was shared by those on the inside of the Memphis establishment when a .357 Magnum was loaned to one of the authors of the book *The Death of Elvis* by a well-connected friend in Memphis *"for his own personal protection"* as they probed deeper into the facts of Elvis Presley's death.

At the time of Presley's murder Elvis was on the outs with Ginger Alden and already had her replacement in mind. Her name was Alicia Kirwin. She was a pretty young thing who was introduced to Elvis by his old friend and local DJ, George Kline.

She was in her early twenties and a teller at a local bank in Memphis. According to many sources Elvis had told Alicia that he and Ginger were finished because she was only after his money.

Alicia Kirwin was sympathetic and could have been the perfect woman for Elvis. In her, Elvis found a companion that wanted to accompany him on his tours, was easy going and far less head strong than Ginger had been.

Presley always had an easier time confiding in women than men and he told Kirwin many inside details of the strangle hold Colonel Parker had on him and who was behind it. In the end, she paid the ultimate price for her knowledge. Shortly after the Presley murder someone at the top realized that she was told far too much about the nuts and bolts of Colonel Parker and his secret partners.

She was found dead of a drug overdose in a hotel, in of all places, Las Vegas, the same town that contributed so much to Elvis Presley's murder. Many questions also surrounded her mysterious death as she was not a drug user.

It appears obvious that there is a monstrous truth surrounding the Elvis Presley murder that people who hold the highest level of power, both legal and illegal, do not want revealed and they are not afraid to flex their all-powerful muscle to keep it quiet.

Exactly how far would they go to cover their tracks and suppress the truth? Apparently farther than anyone had originally imagined. On November 20, 2006, two years after the state and local government rejected Bill Beeny's attempt to have the Presley case reopened with concrete evidence, Alicia Kirwin would be joined in death by another unsuspecting person who had inside knowledge of what really happened.

On that date the *Oxford Eagle* reported that a well-known Elvis Presley researcher, who was to be the keynote speaker at a newly formed, and hopefully annual, Elvis convention was brutally murdered.

His name was Jared Parker (no relation to Colonel Parker), and his keynote speech was going to reveal stunning new facts about the newly uncovered letters from Presley that were now in his possession.

Jared Parker
Used with permission – www.crimescene.com

Parker planned to expose the letters by writing a book on the subject matter of who was threating Presley's life. It appears obvious that the powers behind Elvis Presley's murder were very motivated to keep Mr. Parker silent as he would have exposed them to the world and spawned a huge investigation.

Day in and day out, if you want to find who is at the center of a conspiracy you always follow the shift in power and the shift in profits, and in the Presley case both lead directly to Colonel Parker.

The Colonel knew when he formed Boxcar Enterprises what Presley's ex-wife Priscilla would come to know years later when she formed Elvis Presley Enterprises in 1982; that long after the biggest star in the world had been rubbed out, his image and likeness would still be very lucrative, much like the famed painters in antiquity whose works soared in value after their deaths.

When Parker formed Boxcar Enterprises, he no longer needed Elvis Presley. In fact, to Colonel Parker's wallet, Elvis was better off dead, and that's exactly what the Colonel made him.

This more than explains Parker's curious actions and comments at Elvis' funeral service. *The Colonel,* explains in great detail how many people at the funeral witnessed Parker acting strangely and very distant.

Both friend and celebrity alike saw the Colonel acting stoic and lingering in the back of the room, speaking to no one. He was not with the Presley family as he certainly could have been, and he was doing everything possible to avert his eyes from looking at the casket and seeing the corpse.

Everyone thought that as the final minutes of the viewing came to a close Parker would have arranged to have one final moment with Elvis, but it never happened. He never walked up to the casket or even looked in its direction and when the casket lid closed, Parker was long gone.

Not only were his actions at the funeral disturbing to the guests, his attire drew equal criticism and suspicion. The men at the funeral were all dressed very sharply in black suits and were finely groomed to perfection. This was done to show their respect for their fallen friend. Parker, on the other hand, did no such thing.

He attended the service wearing a wild blue Hawaiian shirt with a baseball cap sitting atop his bushy tufts of wild gray hair. The mere sight of Parker's strange attire and behavior at the funeral service made the blood of the onlookers boil.

Even the many business associates Parker was in constant contact with during the period immediately after the death of Elvis Presley were amazed at how calm and unbothered he seemed to be after the loss of what should have been his closest and longest friend.

After all, he'd reared Elvis' career and watched him blossom into the biggest star in the world. In their 22-year-relationship they had been through just about everything imaginable, but instead of treating Elvis as a son, Parker loathed him. Byron Raphael gave a very telling interview to classicbands.com explaining the situation and the mindset of Colonel Parker:

> "After Elvis died is when most of the money was made. The day of Elvis' funeral, Colonel Parker went to the funeral, never looked in the coffin, turned to Vernon Presley, his father, and said, 'Let's go to work.' Poor Elvis had been with him since he was seventeen years old and those were his only words – 'Let's go to work.' "

No wonder Vernon Presley was so adamant in his assumption that Elvis was murdered, and he ordered a full and thorough investigation. Vernon knew that Elvis' enemies were both close and mounting. The very idea that Parker's could be so cold and callous seemed unimaginable to everyone around him.

It's a coldness that only a Mafia-run, brutal murderer and certified psychopath could produce. This was a man with no feeling of remorse, sensitivity or common decency.

A man whose lust for gambling, power and total control couldn't be fulfilled by one Elvis Presley or twenty Elvis Presleys, and in the end the demon that consumed and ruined Colonel Parker, pulled Elvis Presley, the greatest star the world has even known, down with him.

To Colonel Parker the funeral of Elvis Presley was different than it was for anyone else in America. Every American citizen would have given anything to gain entry to Graceland's private service, but Parker couldn't wait to find the exit.

All he had on his mind was how he could profit from it and the funeral was nothing more than an interruption. There is a quote from Nash's *The Colonel* made by Parker himself that shows what a soulless monster he truly was. In reference to the grief over the loss of Elvis, Parker responded; *"'No, sir. If anyone had seen my eyes mist up for a second they must have had their hands in my pockets.'"*

This sums up what Elvis Presley truly meant to Colonel Tom Parker after all those years together, an object to be discarded like so many hands Parker played and lost at the tables in Las Vegas.

By 1977, the heads of the Mob families who ran the Las Vegas casinos had changed, and no one was going to float Parker his enormous and growing gambling marker anymore.

The new face of Las Vegas wanted their money and Parker had grossly over stayed his welcome along with his IOU's. By the month of Presley's death, Colonel Parker's gambling debt was in excess of 32 million dollars.

With Parker unable to sell Presley's contract just prior to his death and the arrival of the disco era, Elvis Presley became more of an obstacle to Parker's profitability than an asset. Panic stricken for his own life, the Colonel made the necessary arrangements that he needed to make with lightning speed.

Within an hour of Presley's body being placed in the mausoleum Parker was already on an airplane to meet with the owner of Factors Etc Inc, Harry Geisler. Geisler was a self-made merchandising millionaire who, at that time, was handling the sole merchandising for blockbuster movies like Star Wars, Rocky and a few others.

He was also the genius behind those famous posters and T-shirts of Farrah Fawcett that no one could keep in stock. Geisler was an average guy with an above average flare for marketing interesting products to large masses of people and making millions doing it.

Soon the percentages were negotiated, and a royalty between the men was established. In the weeks and months that followed their arrangement made them an untold fortune, just as Colonel Parker had foreseen, and for Parker the glut of hush money and gambling repayment came just in the nick of time.

And so unravels the mystery of Elvis Presley's death. Not a drug overdose, not a suicide and not a death by natural causes. A death well planned and plotted. Murder with all of the true hallmarks of every other famous murder in which the US government and the Mafia families combined evil forces to commit. Murder most foul.

So what's really behind all of the Elvis sightings that crop up all over America? There are two very simple explanations. The first explanation is driven by money while the second is driven by mistaken identity.

With every report of Elvis Presley randomly roaming the countryside being escorted by Bigfoot and the Loch Ness monster, more and more records, posters and various other merchandise flies out the door being replaced by money; lots and lots of money.

The people behind these ridiculous Elvis sightings are the same people who profit from keeping Elvis alive in our minds and our hearts. This foolishness started as a clever ploy by Colonel Parker to keep sales brisk and prostitute the memory of Elvis Presley at our expense and the same ploy continues to this day through its newest whore master, Elvis Presley Enterprises.

Don't believe me? It couldn't be more obvious. Go to www.Graceland.com and look under the Elvis tab. There you will find and entire page dedicated to numerous Elvis sightings and behind every one of them is someone trying, and succeeding, to ring the cash register. As if these people don't make enough money feasting of the specter of the man they have to stoop to this?!

The second explanation driving these Elvis sightings is a bit more honest, and to be honest, I never knew the source of them until I became friends with Suzanna Leigh, Elvis' costar on Paradise Hawaiian Style. Suzanna, who was the goddaughter of legendary film actress Vivian Leigh, who is best known as Scarlett O'Hara in *Gone with The Wind*.

Suzanna told me something that I never would have imagined about the various episodes of Elvis Presley's mistaken identity. The beleaguered Presley made over 30 films in rapid succession at a furious pace that no one human being could withstand. To accomplish these tasks it soon became obvious to Elvis, along with the director, that they needed help.

What they came up with was a way for Elvis to remain in the studio laying down his soundtracks for these movie projects while the film crew could get the movies started in his absence. Suzanna blew my mind when she told me that the first four scenes that she filmed in her movie with Elvis were not with Elvis at all, but with his stage double.

She would go onto tell me that Elvis had doubles in these movies that were surgically altered to look almost exactly like him. In fact they looked so much like him that some of the publicity photos for the movie Paradise Hawaiian Style were not Elvis at all!

When she told me this I was so blown away that I almost didn't believe her, but sure enough, she pointed out the slight differences in their faces which made me a believer. Elvis' face was very chiseled and triangular, while Matt's face, the name of one of the movie double that they used for some of the photos, was very rounded.

Once she told me to look for the Elvis with the jowls in the photos I could easily spot the differences between the men, but you have to really look hard and know what you are looking for.

They were the same build, height and they even moved the same way. As the Presley movie machine began to really heat up and some of the films were completed in a mere 30 days, yet another movie double was needed. His name was John, and he also altered to look like Elvis.

While John was used in more of the fight scenes, Matt was used a little more often in the closer scenes but both men looked almost identical to Elvis. The studio was positively thrilled with their new found assets as they allowed filming to continue while Elvis was elsewhere. This was a tremendous time saver.

These are the men that everyone is seeing in their advanced age and they are assuming that they are Elvis, the real Elvis, when they really aren't. Of all the famous murders that have been planned by the real owners of this country: Sonny Liston, John F. Kennedy, Marilyn Monroe, Martin Luther King Jr., and so many others, Elvis Presley's murder is by far the most masterful because the murder itself has been hidden from the general public for decades while those responsible laugh up their sleeves at his fans.

That's right; they are playing us as fools. The longer they can convince Presley fans to continue to look for a living Elvis ordering Whoppers at Burger King, the longer these *Elvis is Alive* proponents continue to find and attempt to decipher planted and imaginary evidence to throw everyone off track, the less time and logical thought is spent solving this cold-case murder.

As I have said numerous times and in numerous interviews, I met the man that took Elvis' brain out of his head. I interviewed him at length, Elvis Presley is quite dead. I wish he wasn't - but he is. It's beyond time for everyone to let this go and start looking for real evidence, but that will never happen.

Today, the second story of Graceland holds thousands of secrets that are so private no tours, video or television specials have ever been filmed there, and they never will be. Not even Graceland's most loyal and prized employees who have been on the payroll for decades have been able to gain entry to Elvis' house within a house.

Celebrities, US presidents and other dignitaries who have asked for a private tour have been flatly denied, and the reason makes great sense. How many people do you really want trudging through a crime scene? What do they know that they are not telling us? What are they hiding upstairs at Graceland and at the highest levels of government? Everything!

Paralyzed in fear from the top down the local government of Memphis and state government of Tennessee will shrink from the investigation that needs to happen, but most likely never will.

Incredibly, the officials in Shelby County, Tennessee were not the only ones paralyzed in fear. On August 15th 2012 I was invited to appear on two Memphis television shows to talk about the first publication of this book.

At the time, I was a rookie author, and it was one of my first TV appearances, so I was as thrilled as I was nervous. It was the 35th anniversary of Elvis' death and "Elvis Week" was in full swing. The city was buzzing with their annual guest appearances and festivities the likes of which I hadn't seen since my last visit to Disney World.

As my televised interview came to a close and I was leaving the studio to do book signings at a local hotel, I was met in the parking lot by a gigantic black man in a police uniform.

The man was more than a foot taller than me and nearly twice my shoulder width, which is incredible in its own right because I am not small in stature. As he approached, he asked if I was the guy who was just on the air trying to solve Elvis' murder? Thinking that he wanted to buy a book, or something, I said yes.

After my answer, he put his thumb on the top of his pistol, which was holstered, but unsnapped, and said, "if I were you I wouldn't be naming any names." Needless to say, after we parted company, I got the hell out of there as fast as I could and I didn't feel completely safe until I was a few miles away.

Once I reached my destination and mentioned the incident to the hotel clerk, it all started to make sense. The clerk told me what I should have already known but was too ratted by the situation to figure out.

She told me that I was getting too close to the truth and people were getting nervous. It was then that I came to the realization that the man who confronted me was no police officer. I also came to another realization.

I am roughly six feet tall and weigh two hundred and thirty five pounds. I have studied various forms of martial arts for decades, and if that confrontation, which could have escalated into one hell of a fight, made me nervous, I can only imagine how intimidated Suzanna Leigh must have felt when she was dealing with her thugs.

In 1978, Suzanna, also a resident of Memphis, was one of first people to publically assert that Elvis was murdered. She, and others, began to demand that the murder be investigated by the local authorities. It never was, but in return for her public comments, she paid an awful price for the knowledge that she had.

As she pressed Elvis' father, Vernon Presley, to get someone, anyone, to investigate Elvis' murder she would have her brake lines cut, her house broken into and eventually burned down. She would be shot at several times, and she would even have all five of her dogs slaughter by an armed intruder who was looking for her but missed her by only a few minutes.

The message was clear. There was to be no murder investigation into Presley's death, and in the end she was chased out of Tennessee finally residing in the state of Florida.

When I met Suzanna and began to talk freely with her, she told me that there were things that you _can_ say in public, and other things that you _can't_ say. Now I fully understand what she meant and why she said it.

That is the ongoing problem with this line of work. The people who do the greatest amount of research, with the intention of telling the truth, often fly too close to the sun and get burned doing it. Suzanna learned her lesson the hard way, and to a much lesser extent, I learned mine.

It is my sincere hope that someone will officially re-open this cold case and solve it – but it will be someone else. As for me, I am washing my hands and my mind of this murder. It took me five years to research and write the first edition of this book, and five more years to write this edition.

I have done my work, but now it's time for me to move on. I have struggled and toiled with these facts and this forbidden knowledge long enough and I have taken this as far as any author could.

I am putting my untold connection to Elvis aside (and yes, there is an untold story here) because I have an entire book series to finish and other projects that need my time.

To the future investigator, whoever that may be, I will state in advance that they need to start immediately before all of the eye witnesses, evidence, and official accounts are completely lost to the sands of time.

Unfortunately, that is already happening. In 2005, Baptist Memorial Hospital, where Elvis was admitted several times and eventually autopsied, was imploded in the name of progress.

Elvis' nurse, Marion Cocke, was there to watch the implosion and burst into tears at the first blast. It was the end of an era for her, as well as an end to so many memories of her career there. I have no doubt that she was also thinking about Elvis. How could she not be?

It took nearly a year to remove the debris, and with it went key evidence that could have helped an investigator get to the bottom of the murder. Dr. Harold Sexton, one of the doctors at the autopsy, still had tissue samples of Elvis' organs stored in dry ice at that hospital. God only knows what happened to them. It's my guess that they are probably gone now as well.

As mentioned earlier in this book, EMT Ulysses Jones died in 2010 followed months later by the loss of another member of Presley's Memphis Mafia, Lamar Fike. As news of Fike's death came to me it placed even more urgency on the necessity of an investigation, but still nothing happened.

In February of 2013 when I wrote first version of this book I made the mistake of mailing a few copies to newspapers in the New York City area in the hopes that they would print a review of the book.

Shortly thereafter, I received a call from one of them who said that he loved the book but there was no way in hell he would print a review of it because it "almost burnt his fingers." It was just too inflammatory for him and that it "scared him to death."

I won't mention his name, but he seemed to be a decent guy. With a chuckle I apologized to him for not writing about more "important things" like unicorns and rainbows. After a few minutes the call ended on a positive note. He told me that if I ever publish any other books to send them along.

The phone call happened during the month of December 2013. Nine months later, during the month of August 2014, these two publications mysteriously appeared on newsstands worldwide.

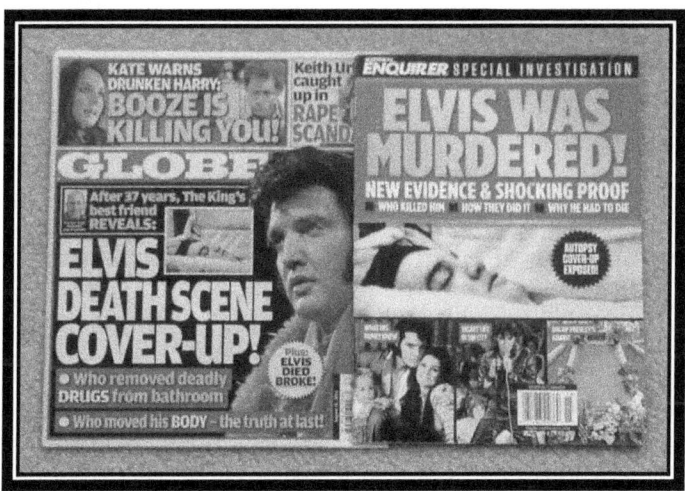

Magically, the contents of my book were 80% stripped, slightly changed, and reprinted under their tabloid's name as if they did all the digging and the legwork. I was so pissed off that I almost climbed out of my skin! I finally understood how exploited Elvis felt under Parker.

Incredibly, one of the magazines quoted my friend Dr. Cyril Wecht, and I knew that the quote didn't come out of his mouth. Within minutes, I had Cyril on the phone and shared the bad news with him. He was equally upset.

I live within a seven-hour drive on New York City and the cerebral, and much calmer, Dr. Wecht, talked me out of taking a road trip to pay these people a visit. Within minutes of that call ending, I had my attorneys on the phone.

They did some brief research and discovered that both the Globe and the National Enquirer are owned by the same company, American Media Inc, and guess where they are located? They are located in New York City and within walking distance of the newspapers that I had sent my book to for their review.

This is how the world works folks. That's a mistake that I certainly work make twice. I won't print the outcome of their copyright thievery of my work but to say that it was an very interesting legal confrontation is an understatement. Remember this: real men fight with lawyers.

Regardless of that mess, I had to ask myself how much more can the truth be punished? I'm fed up with these gigantic conglomerates trying to squash the common person and brainwash them in the process - enough already.

Speaking of gigantic corporations twisting the truth I am equally tired of Priscilla taking all of the credit for saving Graceland. The person named Pricilla Presley ceased to legally exist in 1974 when she was divorced from Elvis, and she took him to court twice to increase her cut of his wealth.

In 1974, she went back to her maiden name of Beaulieu, and was highly motivated to be as far away from Elvis as she could get. Somehow, magically, three years later when Elvis died she was a Presley again? How doe$ that work?

Unlike Suzanna Leigh, who absolutely despises Pricilla, I have nothing against her, but for god sake, please admit, just once on national TV, that there are dozens of highly talented men and women working at Elvis Presley Enterprises (EPE) who make it function and stop taking all of the credit.

While she does make highly intelligent decisions in her executive role she is not the only person running all of those departments and she shouldn't make it sound that way. While she's at it, she can also stop saying bad things about Elvis in the media and in other publications when the man isn't here to defend himself.

Suzanna, who was a frequent guest at the functions in Memphis during "Elvis Week", has many friends who work at EPE and they have commented many times that Priscilla hates Elvis and there isn't even a photo of him on her desk in Graceland. Those are Susanna's words, not mine.

Sadly Priscilla is doing what Elvis never got the opportunity to do, enjoy his wealth in peace. She's the one we should build the shrine to. She drove Elvis crazy with jealousy, cheated on him, divorced him, broke his heart, and then ended up making millions from his image.

All the while she manages to have final word on their divorce decades after his death when he isn't here to refute anything that she says. Well played Priscilla. Is there any justice in this world?

Her latest attempt to contort Elvis' memory for her own monetary gain comes in the form of a suicide note that she claims Elvis had written, which mysteriously made the global headlines, just days before the debut of her new HBO movie, *Elvis Presley: The Searcher.*

The transparent timing of this startling new suicide note and supporting TV special was announced on the heels of Lisa Marie claiming that she has blown through all of Elvis' fortune and the tabloids claiming that she is both pregnant and in drug rehab.

The timing also aligned with Lisa Marie allegedly suing her agent over her lost fortune, Priscilla getting custody of her youngest children and at a time when Graceland's profits were rumored to be dipping. Coincidence? Hardly.

While I am thrilled that Priscilla is working very hard to keep Elvis' image alive, we must realize that she will continue to try and get rich from her marriage to Elvis which ended over four decades ago. In fact she was a Presley less than one tenth of her life but she plays it to perfection.

I'm sure in a few years Graceland will claim that Elvis was really a smurf and then charge everyone a fee to look at the color blue. I guess that's how they reinvent things and there is no one better at it than they are but it's time to see Priscilla for what she really is. She's a very intelligent woman out to profit from the product that she is selling by any means necessary and kudos to her, unfortunately, none of that has anything to do with the truth and it never will.

When I wrote first version of this book I remarked at how terrible it was that Lamar Fike had joined Charlie Hodge, Vernon Presley and Colonel Parker in death, as everything that they knew had been lost forever, and while that is a horrible shame, today, matters are worse.

In 2016, Dr. Nichopolous, a man who was in total agreement that Elvis had been murdered, died of old age and the only thing that remains of his opinion on the subject has been reduced to film footage on my website. Yes, it's there for all to see.

Dr. Nick knew that Geraldo Rivera in his 1979 ABC 20/20 investigation was pushing a phony drug narrative on the unsuspecting American public because ABC needed the ratings to keep 20/20 on the air. It was crap then, and it's crap now.

Dr. Nick also knew that the last toxicology was forged to make it look like there were more drugs were in Presley than actually were. In 1979 Dan Warlick corroborated Dr. Nick's findings that Elvis did not die of a drug overdose and today his story hasn't changed. Warlick is a man of high character. Finally in all of this mess I have managed to find one.

A year after Dr. Nick left us, the sands of time have taken even more of Elvis' Memphis Mafia from us. Red West, Sonny West, Joe Esposito, and Marty Lacker have now died, leaving only a few people who could testify as to what they know.

Later that year I met Suzanna Leigh, who was in the process of writing her own book on the subject. Unfortunately, at the time of our meeting, she was also fighting a courageous battle against stage four liver cancer and although she was winning the battle for more than two years, she would eventually succumb to her illness on the 11th of December.

I will certainly miss Suzanna for the kind and wonderful person that she was, and I will never forget our talks or the unimaginable price that she paid for her telling the truth. She is proof positive that the truth doesn't always set you free; in some cases, it actually imprisons you.

As 2017 turned into 2018 I met three more people who were close to Elvis who have repeatedly told me that he was murdered but have threatened to sue me if I reveal their identities.

This is very frustrating for me because I can't divulge who they are or what I was told. What I can tell you is that all three of them are employed by, you guessed it, EPE. One of them works in the radio field and the other two work at Graceland.

Their inside information alone could blow this case wide open, but they will never say a word publically because it would cost them their jobs and my lips are being forced closed. Again, I must remember Suzanna's advice; there are some things you *can't* say, so you have to let them go.

In late May of 2018 I was traveling through Tennessee and decided to stop in and see Dan Warlick at his law office. In recent years I had forged a friendship with Dan. He greatly respected my work, and was amazed at the evidence that existed outside of the autopsy table that indicated to him that Elvis was murdered.

Although I had fallen out of touch with Dan for several months, as busy people often do, I was really looking forward to this visit in particular. When we last spoke he was trying to find an investigator to solve Elvis' murder - but this visit wasn't to be.

When I called Dan's mobile number to arrange our meeting it was disconnected. Surely this was a mistake. I redialed my phone and to my dismay, I got the same message for a second time.

I thought there must be a problem with his mobile phone so I dialed his office. That number was also disconnected. What the hell is going on here?! To get to the bottom of this mystery I pulled off the road and googled his name. Incredibly, I found his obituary! Dan Warlick died at 69 years old of a heart attack two weeks after our last meeting.

I was furious that no one called to tell me. Then, after a time, my heart sank over the loss of my friend as the inevitable sadness hit me. As I drove through Nashville my mind drifted as I tried to make sense of what had happened. Then I was hit by a tremendous second wave of grief.

Now that Dan's gone, the world has lost all ties to the truth of the original autopsy. Now there will be no investigator to solve Elvis' murder because everything that Dan knew is gone. Now we may never know the answers to the two biggest questions that we had.

First, if it's a medical fact that Elvis Presley was allergic to Codeine, and there was no sign the drugs allergic reaction in Presley's corpse upon Dan Warlick's inspection of his larynx, how did a mega dose of Codeine magically appear in one, and only one, of the three toxicology reports? If Codeine is not in the body – it can't be in the toxicology report. Can someone please explain to me how it got there?

Second, who was behind the forced-promotion of the erroneous (codeine-laden) toxicology report? Why were the results of that third, and final report, selected to be broadcast to the world? This is solely responsible for starting the multi-generational lie that Elvis Presley died of a drug overdose.

Why? Why weren't the first two toxicology reports promoted that showed nothing in his system? If I am wrong about Rivera and his 20/20 team altering the documents to help boost their ratings, then who did it?

Someone is trying very hard to throw the public off the track of the cold case and it has been working exceedingly well for decades. Also, human beings don't exactly have a great reputation for finding or dealing with the truth. Based on their history they excel at mindlessly repeating what they have been told and acting like bobble heads.

Thanks to that, investigative journalism is dead, and society has been reduced to a world full of human canaries who flutter around and vocalize what they have been told without the slightest trace of second-level thinking. But there are a few of us, very few of us, that desire real answers and are less tabloid minded. Are you one of those people?

That's a question that you will have to answer for yourself, but one thing is certain, now that you have read this book, you share the burden of this knowledge. Will you spring into action? The choice is yours.

For Elvis Presley, there is no choice. While his remains lie moldering in his grave a truckload of money is being sucked from the pockets of his loyal fans each year by his ex-wife who has retaken his name for marketing purposes and, who allegedly, hates him.

As for the fans, they flock to Memphis from all corners of the globe and visit Graceland, buying everything that bears his name and image. They stand at attention for hours in candlelight vigils and brave the sweltering heat that August brings to Tennessee without flinching or complaining.

They are good natured, kind, and obedient and their revenue brings corporations like Elvis Presley Enterprises as well as the state of Tennessee billions of dollars which helps drive both the public and private sector economies.

They willingly do all of those things because they know that Elvis Presley was a great man, a loyal man, a God-fearing man and quite possibly the most generous person that ever walked the earth.

Elvis' fans are doing their part, it is not asking too much for cold case investigators to do theirs. After more than forty years of unwavering loyal homage, Elvis fans everywhere have earned the right to hear the whole truth.

Exactly how deep does the rabbit hole really go? All the way down to the dirge of a poor kid from Tupelo, Mississippi whose stage performances captivated a generation and motivated the full power of the FBI and Mafia to murder him.

While writing this book I was constantly reminded of a quote by Michael Corleone in Francis Ford Coppola's epic film, *The Godfather II*: "If anything in this life is certain - if history has taught us anything - it's that you can kill anybody." How amazingly prophetic that statement is.

If Elvis Presley magically sprang back to life tomorrow and wanted to perform, they would murder him again and probably not tell a soul. They would do anything to keep the money and the cover up going.

And so, the burden of this knowledge has been passed on to you, and the commission to those who seek the truth officially begins. The truth might hurt, but it should never be hidden, and I write to ensure that it never will be.

This volume and the volumes that follow solve histories mysteries and make great conversation pieces. For all of your gift giving needs visit the book series website.
www.whomurderedbooks.com

www.ingramcontent.com/pod-product-compliance
Lightning Source LLC
Chambersburg PA
CBHW071649090426
42738CB00009B/1467